CHRISTOPHER HITCHENS

CHRISTOPHER HITCHENS
THE LAST INTERVIEW
and OTHER CONVERSATIONS

with an introduction by STEPHEN FRY

MELVILLE HOUSE
BROOKLYN • LONDON

CHRISTOPHER HITCHENS: THE LAST INTERVIEW AND OTHER CONVERSATIONS

First Melville House printing: December 2017

Melville House Publishing		8 Blackstock Mews
46 John Street	and	Islington
Brooklyn, NY 11201		London N4 2BT

ISBN: 978-1-61219-672-5

Printed in the United States of America
10 9 8 7 6 5 4 3 2 1

A catalog record for this book is available from the Library of Congress.

CONTENTS

INTRODUCTION

STEPHEN FRY

When friends die before their time they are missed in expected ways: memories of their company, the echo of their voice, the flash in their eyes, the rumble of their laugh and the swing of their gait can haunt and torment us. Personal quirks, mannerisms and traits represent a light that has gone out. But sometimes a person is missed for more pressing, selfish reasons. The loss of Christopher Hitchens is felt by those who knew him for all the foregoing, but by a huge tranche of those who never met him because the acuity, insight, originality and power of his mind and language are more urgently needed now than they have ever been.

Hitchens ("the Hitch" or "Christopher" but never, never, unless you wanted a verbal slap that could cause tears to spring to your eyes, *never* "Chris") was crammed with accomplishments. He had an extraordinary memory, an impossibly fast and efficient ability to assemble information, synthesize ideas and express them on the fly in elegant, forceful and original language that could still a hall and quell an opponent. How someone who socialized, drank, dined, debated, broadcast, wrote and traveled so much also found time to read and think so widely and deeply was a mystery that puzzled even those who knew him well. There were gaps in his knowledge—his ignorance of serious music and almost all sport was as profound as his mastery of literature, history, philosophy, art, architecture, scientific theory, politics and world affairs. He could quote Larkin, Baudelaire and Billy Wilder with the accuracy of a fanboy and the next minute anatomize the nuanced variations of doctrine within Luxemburgist theory, the Pelagian heresy or Mevlevi Sufism.

The role of the public intellectual has had a fraught history in the United States and Great Britain. We look with envy to the respected position such figures seem to occupy in France, Italy and Spain. Some years ago the vituperative high-end bickering of Gore Vidal and William Buckley could entertain millions on network TV. Christopher, in his pomp, popped up on smaller niche stations like CNN and MSNBC but had at least the advantage of those appearances proliferating on YouTube and social media gaining him devoted followers—and his share of fierce detractors.

He made his bones and developed his chops (two phrases he would have hated) in the adversarial world of British left wing political discourse, where reflex, confidence, volume and unswerving conviction were the minimum requirements for

survival. Starting out as a stout but idiosyncratically hetero-
dox Trotskyist (he disavowed "Trotsky*ite*") Hitchens trod
the well-worn path of sixties fellow-traveler, visiting eastern
bloc satellite states as well as the expected Latin American,
middle-eastern and Asian flash points. He mastered the com-
plexities of Vietnam, Cyprus, Palestine, Central America,
South Africa, Cuba and the Balkans, espousing just the
views you would expect of a leftist forged in the fires of street
demos, student sit-ins and fevered meeting rooms.

But with a depth of education and interests too broad
to confine him to dogma and doctrine, and a pride and rigor
too great to allow him the soft comforts of liberalism, he soon
established himself in the role of Christopher the Contrarian,
a persona he would take to the grave. In the 1980s and 90s
loyal journalists and commentators of the left, (whom he
was not above designating "the Mediahideen") watched in
alarm as his almost animal dislike and distrust of all things
Clintonian, fueled by his absolute disgust for fundamentalist
Islam, seemed to propel him ideologically into the arms of
George W. and the Republicans. He was nobody's spokesman but his own and those who presumed to second guess
his views on anything from jazz to Jerusalem would invite
the lash of his contemptuous tongue, yet nonetheless his last
two decades on the planet saw him as much occupied with
defending himself to erstwhile confreres of the left as with
combating his old enemies on the right. He was no Norman
Podhoretz, but to some it was beginning to look uncomfort-
ably, in *Animal Farm* terms, as if the pig was now wearing . . .
if not trousers then at least perhaps culottes. He coped with
these assaults with all the firepower his rhetoric could bring

to bear, even if it did sometimes make him look a little like an enthroned tyrant fly-whisking at gnats.

Despite his endearing deployment of an old-fashioned "sir" or "madam" when crossing swords with an adversary, Christopher in debate mode was never what you might call cuddly. Fond of him as I was, filled with admiration for his integrity, courage and intellectual honesty as one could not fail to be, in his presence I always found myself in awe and—truth be told—more than a little timid. He knew more than me about almost everything; no matter how much Johnny Walker Black Label had gone down him he thought with a cleaner, clearer, sharper mind and always had far less truck with compromise or accommodation. I am mostly a hand-wringing milquetoast who likes people to get along. Christopher had little patience with my kind of softness and the drift into moral cowardice that it can engender. I would not presume to call him my Jiminy Cricket, but access to him kept me kind of honest. Another selfish reason to miss him.

From his perspective recent history represented not a triumph of the right but a failure of the left. This is why his absence is felt so keenly today by all who value intelligent, informed, passionate public discourse. We want him to tell us what to think, or at least how to respond to all that is happening in our sublunary post-Hitchens world. We need to know how he would have engaged with an America led by Trump and a Britain riven by Brexit. It is clear what he thought of Hillary Clinton, but what would he have made of Bernie Sanders and Jeremy Corbyn? Would he have respected or fiendishly triggered the pampered campus darlings in their safe spaces? How would he have reacted to the imperial rise of the silicon valley tycoons and the oncoming tsunami of robotics and AI?

Christopher's latter years were dominated, in the public's imagination at least, by many well-publicized assaults on religion. Those written and spoken philippics, so forensically brilliant and astutely reasoned are probably what he will (at least in the short term) be best remembered for. The so-called New Atheist movement will turn on fortune's wheel as all things do, but it would be a shame if people failed to understand Christopher's real beef with churches, mosques and temples. He happened not to believe in a god, but that was a side issue. The visceral distrust of unwarranted authority and instinctive feel for the exploited that took him as a student from the killing fields of Indochina to the barrios of San Salvador also fired his contempt for popes and horoscopes, clerisy and heresy, Brahmas and lamas, prelates and zealots, friars, liars, shamans, laymen and the puffed and preposterous panoply of hermeneuts and exegetes to whom Truth and The Way have been revealed.

Combative, merciless and unyielding, the hard core of Hitchens was leavened by a fizzing yeast of humor. Being funny and finding the world funny were not incidental to him. The places of Waugh, Wodehouse and Wilde in his pantheon were central and defining. Only serious people have a sense of humor, only those who best understand the world can make us laugh.

To the last Christopher boldly and hilariously repudiated the possibilities of any afterlife save the kind represented by the publication of books like the one in your hands now. This welcome edition of the Last Interview series allows us to hear that marvelous voice again and for it to refuel our own engines of advocacy, argument and resistance.

Like his hero Orwell, Christopher's mode of address to the political, cultural and social world stands outside the temporary issues of his time, whose provisional details and contingent concerns already seem strangely distant. He teaches us that reason, learning, engagement and commitment can turn tides. The Hitchens manner can never die.

HITCHENS ON THE MEDIA

INTERVIEW BY CARL RUTAN
C-SPAN
FEBRUARY 10, 1987

RUTAN: Christopher Hitchens, a Washington correspondent, uh, with *The Nation*, you write a column for them every two weeks. There are lots and lots of TV talk shows that news junkies can watch to get information or hear analysis. What do you think of these talk shows?

HITCHENS: Or to watch their friends, or to see how the press sort of massages itself in a narcissistic manner. I, um, I wrote a piece about it recently for *Harper's Magazine* saying that the, really the level now of TV discussion of ideas and politics has become humiliatingly low, that it's the province of various, well what I call, repertory company of pundits, who take themselves far too seriously, who take each other far too seriously, and are taken by too many viewers more seriously than they deserve because these programs are very light minded, very frivolous. Usually they're contrived, though they pretend not to be—the fix is in. There are built-in limits to what's going to be said or can be said. And that it's, I suggest towards the end of my thesis—maybe for this reason— that the culture of journalism in Washington has become so sycophantic. The president didn't have a really tough press conference until he was six years into his, uh, presidency and when the country was entering into tremendous crisis, only then did he start getting tough questions.

RUTAN: This is the article *[holds up copy of* Harper's Magazine *to the camera]* that appears in the recent issue of *Harper's*, and you call it "Blabscam," or an editor might have given it that— did you call it this or did some editor give it that title?

HITCHENS: I must say, I think it was Lewis Lapham, the editor. It's a clever one, I'd like to claim credit for it.

RUTAN: "Blabscam, TV's rigged political talk shows" by you, Christopher Hitchens. "Blabscam" suggests a scandal. Is it really a scandal?

HITCHENS: Yeah, I think it's a scandal. I think it's a crying shame. *[Coughs]* I mean, I've been now on *The McLaughlin Group*, which probably some of your customers watch too, on, um, *It's Your Business*—on most of these shows. The only one, you may be touched to see, I don't mention as being a fix is, um, this show and I guess I could have also, um, mentioned *Firing Line* which I've been on, William Buckley's program which, again, I wouldn't include. I mean, in both these shows, if you walk off the set and think, "Damn, I wish I had been able to say this or I wish I had remembered to say that," it's your own fault. You had the chance to. With the others it's all heavily confined occasions for the chairman to show off usually. Um, and unspoken agreement among the parties that certain awkward things won't get mentioned at all. Um, so people are just really role playing.

RUTAN: Now, uh, for your appearance on C-Span this

morning, you get one of these [taps mug with pen] handsome mugs we are drinking coffee out of this morning—

HITCHENS: Ah.

RUTAN: Do you get paid for the other shows, the other talk shows around Washington?

HITCHENS: Um, *McLaughlin* pays.

RUTAN: What do they pay? How much?

HITCHENS: Um, I can't remember. I think if you're a regular, it's about $500 a shot. I think I got $350 as a guest. Um, [clears throat] the other ones don't. I mean, the other ones, journalists would pay to go on because you are taken very seriously if you're seen, you know, asking a toadying question to the secretary of state on one of the Sunday morning shows. So, it enhances your marketability. What, um, what is in it for journalists, is the tremendous increase in the rate they can charge for public speaking. If you are on the Brinkley show or something, then you'll get a call from the league of women flower arrangers in Des Moines and you can, instead of accepting their $500, you can say, "Well, I don't usually get out of bed for more than, uh, for less than two grand." And the marketability goes up in that way. TV really helps you out.

RUTAN: Let's talk about the, uh, three shows that are so widely watched on Sunday mornings, and I'm sure C-Span viewers, who read lots of newspapers, probably watch those shows. Must admit that I do. And I'm going to hold up your article from *Harper's*, dateline Washington, an interesting story about how these shows are put together and how these shows consistently get top government officials. Dateline Washington, "In the White House press office, there sits a woman named Denny E. Brisley. You may not know Ms. Brisley. But if you watch the Sunday morning political chat shows, you know her work. To her falls the job of producing and editing the key segments of *This Week with David Brinkley*, *Meet the Press*, and *Face the Nation*." Now, how is it that a White House official edits key segments of those three shows?

HITCHENS: The White House can decide who they are going to put up in a given week and they can tell administration officials not to go on the air that day, and they can tell others that they should go forward and carry the torch for the line of the week—whatever it may be, 'cause it now keeps changing so often. They can then get the three shows to bid against each other, for whoever is the most famous or prominent administration spokesman that week. And what that means is that these shows are not going to have you and me—critical independent minds as we are—on. When the White House rings up they say, "Well, so you'd like Mr. McFarland?" and, um, they say yes. And they say "Well, you know, CBS is looking for him too. Let me see, well what questions were you thinking of asking him? Who is, uh, who is going to be the panel?" Producers can learn quite quickly that you're not going to make trouble for the guy; otherwise you'll always be at the end of the totem pole that week. So, what looks like competition between the three networks is in fact a competition to please and to be bland, and not to outbid for getting the story, but outbid for getting the ratings-building figure. Now I say that is a scam, in the sense that it is a corruption of journalism. Yeah, and it is the reason why, um, the administration has been able to have such a tremendously easy ride over the last six years. And I say that, of course, as a political opponent of the administration, but I think it's not in the interests of people who support the administration—to have it go uncriticized, it's bad for it. It's bad for our trade of journalism too. So that's really the essence of what I'm saying, and I remembered one of those producers of one of those shows—I won't say which one—saying to me, "I'm sick of having Larry Speakes being the chief producer for Sunday morning TV in this country." And that's really what the situation was.

RUTAN: You talk it, and you interviewed, uh, Ms. Brisley, is that correct?

HITCHENS: I, uh, no. I didn't interview Ms. Brisley. I, um, *The Nation* is incredibly low in the administration's scale of priorities when it comes to giving interviews. We're never called at press conferences; they never call us back. I mean, that kind of thing. But those words are direct quotes that she gave to a friend of mine.

RUTAN: The quotes from Ms. Brisley to your friend are

basically saying, "'It's all done in a very sensitive, diplomatic type language. Things are said, but not said.' Among the things 'said' in this unspoken dialogue is something along these lines, 'Don't even think about having X on the panel of questioners or we'll go to another network with the secretary and you'll look small.'"

HITCHENS: Yeah.

RUTAN: So they even do it with journalists that might be asking tough questions of a member of the cabinet.

HITCHENS: Yeah. I mean, it's a very small pool of people. I mean, look it's like when, uh, I remember—I think it was the night of the bombing of Libya, um, a moment of extreme controversy in American life, in public life, and in American relations with the rest of the world. You know, *Nightline* calls up its list of impartial experts, and these are always the same people—Henry Kissinger, sometimes Jeane Kirkpatrick. Until very recently Michael Ledeen—who turns out to have been a man who was an expert on terrorism only in the sense of being a man bargaining with terrorists and swapping hostages for weapons with terrorists—was unabashedly on the television every week as NSC terrorism expert. So the definition of "expert" they had was, A, very narrow and, B, one that generally fit the government's perspective on the issue. So that one had a tremendously conformist sense of politics and of debate transmitted into millions of homes without anyone really knowing the name of this woman in the White House press office, Denny Brisley, whose job it is to keep the thing

smooth and prevent any rough questions or rough questioners from breaking it.

RUTAN: Is it possible for Ms. Denny Brisley or someone in
the White House or in the White House press office to keep
a critic of the Reagan administration off the shows by simply
saying, "If you have them on, we won't give you the secretary
and we will give the secretary to your competitors."

HITCHENS: As I say, and as she says, it's done in a sensitive,
diplomatic manner. After a while, I mean, any producer
whose got any sense of himself at all will know what to do
without being told. Let's put it like that.

RUTAN: *[holds up newspaper]* Let's take a look at who was on
the, uh, TV talk shows last week, they do get a lot of publicity,
and I'm looking at Monday's *USA Today* and there's a little
story they have right here [points to newspaper] in the fold.
Excuse me, I should have ironed this first.

[Hitchens laughs off camera]

In the "TV Talk" section, uh, it says that "Henry Kissinger
and Cyrus Vance—fresh from visiting Mikhail Gorbachev—
say Soviets are serious about arms control." They were on
Meet the Press, and then Secretary of State George Shultz
was on ABC's *This Week with David Brinkley*, and then Iran
ambassador to the United Nations, um, "denied on CBS's
Face the Nation that Iran is backing the religious extremists."
So that's a look at some of the people who were on. Also was

Senator, uh, Sam Nun from Georgia talking about the president's strategic defense initiative. How affective are these, for whether you're a Democrat—like a Senator Sam Nun—or a Republican—like Secretary of State Shultz, how affective are these Sunday morning talk shows for getting your message out, getting your message to the people?

HITCHENS: Well I think for getting the message out, um, they're reasonably good because on the whole the programs are tribunes for these characters. I mean they are asked questions in a very respectful tone of voice, they asked, uh, "Senator what's your opinion on this, can you tell us more about that?" It's all done in an extremely polite way and yet you still have the administration claiming that it has an adversarial relationship with the media. Um, more important though, I think is name recognition. You know, if you are on there, it means that you've been in a sense mentioned, you've caught the eye of the people who make and break reputations in Washington. And, um, that's also true of course if you've been invited on to be a questioner, that's a sign you've entered a certain sanctum of a certain club. Um, people inside these clubs on the whole are not interested in letting in any fresh air or any noise from the street.

RUTAN: You also go on in your article "Blabscam," in *Harper's*, to talk about *The McLaughlin Group*, which you call the McLaugh . . . McLaughlin . . . McLaughian—excuse me.

HITCHENS: The McLaughian, yes.

RUTAN: McLaughian. Why do you call it that? Why do you say that?

HITCHENS: Because the McLaughian is, um, an unserious show. A sort of a poke at a shouting and screaming match between people who pretend to be representing opposing opinions, who in fact share most of their assumptions, are close personal friends and colleagues, and put on a show really for suckers—as if they are Washington insiders having a knock down, drag out fight. And I think probably some people think that's what they're getting when they watch it and they're not.

RUTAN: It's not an unrehearsed—

HITCHENS: By no means unrehearsed.

RUTAN: —dialogue?

HITCHENS: No. I mean, they . . . it advertises itself as unrehearsed, but one is put through an intensive course of preparation when the, uh, when one is a guest or participant in the show.

RUTAN: This is, uh, an advertisement in, uh, *New Republic* and you may have seen it for what's called "Spontaneous Combustion" and it's about *The McLaughlin Group*—it's a little advertisement. You would say that "Spontaneous Combustion" is not a very accurate to—

HITCHENS: It's not, it's certainly not. I don't think it's very combustible, but it is certainly not spontaneous. No.

RUTAN: Let's, let's talk about the people. You've appeared on this program and the people who appear on this and many of our viewers are familiar with it. What do you think of, um, of some of these people? Robert Novak, starting off on the side [points to Novak in the advertisement].

HITCHENS: Well Robert Novak is a shill for the administration, I mean, his column—which is syndicated in quite a number of papers—is simply the, uh, dog biscuits and scraps that are thrown to him by Reaganites, sometimes to leak against each other, sometimes to leak against the Democrats, or Congress, or the press. And he just shoves it in and passes it on. So, he's a conduit really. That's all.

RUTAN: What about Morton Kon—

HITCHENS: Uh, pretending to be a fearless, investigative, you know, don't tread on me type. Don't believe a word of it.

RUTAN: What about Morton Kondracke?

HITCHENS: Morton Kondracke is, I would say, your classic liberal, ambitious defector. The guy says, "I use to be liberal and now I've seen the light. I'm very much more grownup now. I'm much more grown-up than I look, for a start. And I'm much cleverer than I look too, and sound. And, um, I've been through these fires of conversion and now I've

,seen that absolutely this is the way it ought to be. You know, you should have people like Ronald Reagan in charge and I can't think why I didn't see it before." Still, as it were, selling the shards of his liberal past—that's an old game too.

RUTAN: How, how do you—

HITCHENS: To hear him talk, you'd think he was the first person ever to have thought of it.

RUTAN: When you were on *The McLaughlin Group*, how were you prepared? What happened before you went on, after?

HITCHENS: You get prepared first by the host himself, a long chat sounding you out, you know, "What do you think about this? What do you think about that?" Then, if it's going to be that Sunday, you get a long telephone call from one of his staffers saying, "Look, these are gonna be the topics"—at least, this is Thursday, this is what the topics are going to be, they may change—"This is the order in which they'll come to you and ask you your questions. When you cue out, they are going to go to Mort. So be ready to do it in that order and then it'll be reverse order on the next question, and the next question will be South Korea." Now on the morning of the taping, they call you and go through all of that again, usually with some changes 'cause there's almost always something in that day's papers that they want to put in. So you go through it again: what the questions will be, what are the topics, and in what order you'll be asked them. Then you sit in your chair and the lights go up and they say, "A spontaneous, unrehearsed show."

[Rutan laughs]

And I remember thinking, "Geez," um, as I sat in my chair, "that's a bit much." And that's only an extreme example, I think, of the way in which, um, this club-land conception of politics dominates most of the TV shows.

RUTAN: You also, in your article "Blabscam," talk about CNN's show *Crossfire*, another, uh, vigorous exchange of ideas and issues. You talk about Robert Novak and you say that one of their producers told you, "Go easy on Bob Novak that evening or bid farewell to *Crossfire*."

HITCHENS: That's right.

RUTAN: What took place in that—

HITCHENS: In fact, I was on . . . the other host on *Crossfire* is a man called Tom Braden, who is allegedly a liberal, actually he is about as liberal as Sam Nun is, I would say. He's certainly not as liberal on his wing as Novak is conservative on his. But, um, for a couple of evenings he was unwell, so I was promoted from being a guest to a guest host. So I sat in the opposite chair and helped to co-host the program. And Novak, as you know if you've seen him, is a man with poisonously bad manners and likes to get other people to lose their temper, and can dish it out but can't take it. So I tried to repay him in his own coin one evening as a co-host, and when I came in the next day they said, "Look, if you don't give an undertaking not to do that again, you're out because he won't come on with you." Now, I wrote to Ted Turner, who runs the network, and I said, "Look, is it by your wish or with your knowledge that one of the participants in this alleged argument every night is also the umpire, the referee? Because that is not how the show advertises itself." *Crossfire* means no holds barred, right? Got a reply, a rather evasive one, from Turner's brother, um, my phone stopped ringing from that studio. I don't want to make myself out to be the guy who's too hot for TV, otherwise I wouldn't be sitting here.

[They laugh]

I'm saying, actually, that it doesn't take very much for them to say, "No he's outside the brackets of what's acceptable. This is all making us uncomfortable, let's go back to the people we know and the viewers are comfortable with. Let's still call it *Crossfire*, but let's make sure that actually the gloves are right on all the time."

RUTAN: You obviously have a heavy British accent, or a light one—pleasant British accent, whatever. What's it like in England? Are there shows like this, and are they prearranged and choreographed as you've described these? Or are there true *Crossfires* and true *McLaughlin Groups*?

HITCHENS: Choreography is a good word. Well I haven't, I was born in Britain, I haven't lived there for a long time now. I'm not sure I can give you all that good of an answer. There is a very—what you might call—respectable overlay to everything in Britain and, um, especially with the BBC, they're fairly careful. You do have in Britain a more parliamentary tradition, and that's reflected in the television shows. We know that Margaret Thatcher has to go to the House of Commons twice a week and, for half an hour, answer any questions thrown at her without any preparation, and be booed if she gives a bad answer—very good discipline for a politician. I don't believe Reagan could do it for a day, for example. And uh, that tradition is carried over a bit into our press conferences, which are not fixed as the White House one is. There isn't a seating plan, there isn't a map on, as there is on Reagan's podium, so he can go to people in prearranged order. All that, which people don't see when they watch them.

RUTAN: European press, rude and surly in comparison to what you see in the American press core—

HITCHENS: Yeah.

RUTAN: —and the White House news conferences?

HITCHENS: Yeah, yeah. The trade off for that is that most of the European press is run by various, uh, boldly declared political interests—they don't pretend to be objective. In this country there is a culture of objectivity, a pretense of it. I mean, I think it makes for boring journalism, and sometimes dishonest, but there is the ambition at least to be fair.

[Call-in portion of the show begins]

HITCHENS
ON MOTHER TERESA

INTERVIEW BY MATT CHERRY
FREE INQUIRY
FALL 1996

Below, Matt Cherry, executive director of the Council for Secular Humanism, interviews Christopher Hitchens about his book *The Missionary Position: Mother Teresa in Theory and Practice* and his television program, which strongly criticized Mother Teresa. The interview recapitulates the most devastating critiques of Mother Teresa ever made. It also gives a very telling account by a leading journalist into the U.S. media's great reluctance to criticize religion and religious leaders.

As *Free Inquiry* was going to press, we heard that Mother Teresa was suffering from heart trouble and malaria and there was concern about her chances of survival. It was, therefore, suggested to the editors that it would be inappropriate to print an interview that contains criticism of Mother Teresa's work and influence. However, in view of the media's general failure to investigate the work of Mother Teresa or to publish critical comments about her, the editors felt it important to proceed with the publication of this revealing interview.

Christopher Hitchens is "Critic at Large" for *Vanity Fair*, writes the Minority Report column for *The Nation*, and is a frequent guest on current affairs and commentary television programs. He has written numerous books on international current affairs, including *Blood, Class, and Nostalgia: Anglo-American Ironies*.

CHERRY: According to polls, Mother Teresa is the most respected woman in the world. Her name is a byword for selfless dedication in the service of humanity. So why are you picking on this sainted old woman?

HITCHENS: Partly because that impression is so widespread. But also because the sheer fact that this is considered unquestionable is a sign of what we are up against, namely the problem of credulity. One of the most salient examples of people's willingness to believe anything if it is garbed in the appearance of holiness is the uncritical acceptance of the idea of Mother Teresa as a saint by people who would normally be thinking—however lazily—in a secular or rational manner. In other words, in every sense it is an unexamined claim.

It's unexamined journalistically—no one really takes a look at what she does. And it is unexamined as to why it should be she who is spotlighted as opposed to many very selfless people who devote their lives to the relief of suffering in what we used to call the "Third World." Why is it never mentioned that her stated motive for the work is that of proselytization for religious fundamentalism, for the most extreme interpretation of Catholic doctrine? If you ask most people if they agree with the pope's views on population, for example, they say they think they are rather extreme. Well here's someone whose life's work is the propagation of the most extreme version of that.

That's the first motive. The second was a sort of journalistic curiosity as to why it was that no one had asked any serious questions about Mother Teresa's theory or practice. Regarding her practice, I couldn't help but notice that she had rallied to the side of the Duvalier family in Haiti, for instance, that she had taken money—over a million dollars—from Charles Keating, the Lincoln Savings and Loans swindler, even though it had been shown to her that the money was stolen; that she has been an ally of the most reactionary forces in India and in many other countries; that she has campaigned recently to prevent Ireland from ceasing to be the only country in Europe with a constitutional ban on divorce, that her interventions are always timed to assist the most conservative and obscurantist forces.

CHERRY: Do you think this is because she is a shrewd political operator or that she is just naive and used as a tool by others?

HITCHENS: I've often been asked that. And I couldn't say from real acquaintance with her which view is correct, because I've only met her once. But from observing her I don't think that she's naive. I don't think she is particularly intelligent or that she has a complex mind, but I think she has a certain cunning.

Her instincts are very good: she seems to know when and where she might be needed and to turn up, still looking very simple. But it's a long way from Calcutta to Port au Prince airport in Haiti, and it's a long way from the airport to the presidential palace. And one can't just, in your humble way and dressed in a simple sari, turn up there. Quite a lot of things have to be arranged and thought about and allowed for in advance. You don't end up suddenly out of sheer simple naiveté giving a speech saying that the Duvalier family love the poor. All of that involves quite a high level of planning and calculation. But I think the genius of it is to make it look simple.

One of Mother Teresa's biographers—almost all the books written about her are by completely uncritical devotees—says, with a sense of absolute wonderment, that when Mother Teresa first met the pope in the Vatican, she arrived by bus dressed only in a sari that cost one rupee. Now that would be my definition of behaving ostentatiously. A normal person would put on at least her best scarf and take a taxi. To do it in the way that she did is the reverse of the simple path. It's obviously theatrical and calculated. And yet it is immediately written down as a sign of her utter holiness and devotion. Well, one doesn't have to be too cynical to see through that.

CHERRY: You point out that, although she is very open about promoting Catholicism, Mother Teresa has this reputation of holiness amongst many non-Catholics and even secular people. And her reputation is based upon her charitable work for the sick and dying in Calcutta. What does she actually do there? What are her care facilities like?

HITCHENS: The care facilities are grotesquely simple: rudimentary, unscientific, miles behind any modern conception of what medical science is supposed to do. There have been a number of articles—I've collected some more since my book came out—about the failure and primitivism of her treatment of lepers and the dying, of her attitude towards medication and prophylaxis. Very rightly is it said that she tends to the dying, because if you were doing anything but dying she hasn't really got much to offer.

This is interesting because, first, she only proclaims to be providing people with a Catholic death, and, second, because of the enormous amounts of money mainly donated to rather than raised by her Order. We've been unable to audit this—no one has ever demanded an accounting of how much money has flowed in her direction. With that money she could have built at least one absolutely spanking new, modern teaching hospital in Calcutta without noticing the cost.

The facilities she runs are as primitive now as when she first became a celebrity. So that's obviously not where the money goes.

CHERRY: How much money do you reckon she receives?

HITCHENS: Well, I have the testimony of a former very active member of her Order who worked for her for many years and ended up in the office Mother Teresa maintains in New York City. She was in charge of taking the money to the bank. She estimates that there must be $50 million in that bank account alone. She said that one of the things that began to raise doubts in her mind was that the Sisters always had to go around pretending that they were very poor and they couldn't use the money for anything in the neighborhood that required alleviation. Under the cloak of avowed poverty they were still soliciting donations, labor, food, and so on from local merchants. This she found as a matter of conscience to be offensive.

Now if that is the case for one place in New York, and

since we know what huge sums she has been given by institutions like the Nobel Peace committee, other religious institutions, secular prize-giving organizations, and so on, we can speculate that if this money was being used for the relief of suffering we would be able to see the effect.

CHERRY: So the $50 million is a very small portion of her wealth?

HITCHENS: I think it's a very small portion, and we should call for an audit of her organization. She carefully doesn't keep the money in India because the Indian government requires disclosure of foreign missionary organizations' funds.

I think the answer to questions about her wealth was given by her in an interview where she said she had opened convents and nunneries in 120 countries. The money has simply been used for the greater glory of her order and the building of dogmatic, religious institutions.

CHERRY: So she is spending the money on her own order of nuns? And that order will be named after her?

HITCHENS: Both of those suggestions are speculation, but they are good speculation. I think the order will be named after her when she becomes a saint, which is also a certainty: she is on the fast track to canonization and would be even if we didn't have a pope who was manufacturing saints by the bushel. He has canonized and beatified more people than eight of his predecessors combined.

CHERRY: Hence the title of your book: *The Missionary Position*.

HITCHENS: That has got some people worked up. Of the very, very few people who have reviewed this book in the United States, one or two have objected to that title on the grounds that it's "sophomoric." Well, I think that a triple entendre requires a bit of sophistication.

CHERRY: And your television program in the United Kingdom was called *Hell's Angel*.

HITCHENS: Yes, very much over my objection, because I thought that that name had not even a single entendre to it. I wanted to call it "Sacred Cow." The book is the television program expanded by about a third. The program was limited by what we could find of Mother Teresa's activities recorded on film. In fact, I was delighted by how much of her activity was available on film: for example, her praising the Albanian dictator Enver Hoxha. There is also film of her groveling to the Duvaliers: licking the feet of the rich instead of washing the feet of the poor. But *60 Minutes* demanded a price that was greater than the whole cost of the rest of the production. So we had to use stills.

CHERRY: How did Mother Teresa become such a great symbol of charity and saintliness?

HITCHENS: Her break into stardom came when Malcolm Muggeridge—a very pious British political and social pundit—adopted her for his pet cause. In 1969, he made a very famous film about her life—and later a book—called *Something Beautiful for God*. Both the book and the film deserve the label hagiography.

Muggeridge was so credulous that he actually claimed that a miracle had occurred on camera while he was making the film. He claimed that a mysterious "kindly light" had appeared around Mother Teresa. This claim could easily be exploded by the testimony of the cameraman himself: he had some new film stock produced by Kodak for dark or difficult light conditions. The new stock was used for the interview with Mother Teresa. The light in the film looked rather odd, and the cameraman was just about to say so when Muggeridge broke in and said, "It's a miracle, it's divine light."

CHERRY: Are we all victims of the Catholic public relations machine? Or has the West seized upon Mother Teresa as salve for its conscience?

HITCHENS: Well, you are giving me my answer in your question. For a long time the church was not quite sure what to do about her. For example, when there was the Second Vatican Council, in the 1960s, there was an equivalent meeting for the Catholics of the Indian subcontinent in Bombay. Mother Teresa turned up and said she was absolutely against any reconsideration of doctrine. She said we don't need any new thinking or reflection, what we need is more work and more faith. So she has been recognized as a difficult and dogmatic woman by the Catholics in India for a long time.

I think there were others in the church who suspected

she was too ambitious, that she wouldn't accept discipline, that she wanted an order of her own. She was always petitioning to be able to go off and start her own show. Traditionally, the church has tended to suspect that kind of excessive zeal. I think it was an entirely secular breakthrough sponsored by Muggeridge, who wasn't then a Catholic.

So it wasn't the result of the propaganda of the Holy Office. But when the Catholic church realized it had a winner on its hands, it was quick to adopt her. She is a very great favorite of the faithful and a very good advertisement to attract non-believers or non-Catholics. And she's very useful for the current pope as a weapon against reformists and challengers within the church.

As to why those who would normally consider themselves rationalists or skeptics have fallen for the Mother Teresa myth, I think there is an element of post-colonial condescension involved, in that most people have a slightly bad conscience about "the wretched of the Earth" and they are glad to feel that there are those who will take action. Then also there is the general problem of credulity, of people being willing—once a reputation has been established—to judge people's actions by that reputation instead of the reputation by that action.

CHERRY: Why do you think no other major media before you had exposed Mother Teresa?

HITCHENS: I'm really surprised by it. And also I'm surprised that no one in our community—that of humanists, rationalists, and atheists—had ever thought of doing it either.

There's a laziness in my profession, of tending to make the mistake I just identified of judging people by their reputation. In other words, if you call Saudi Arabia a "moderate Arab state" that's what it becomes for reportorial purposes. It doesn't matter what it does, it's a "moderate state." Similarly for Mother Teresa: she became a symbol for virtue, so even in cartoons, jokes, movies, and television shows, if you want a synonym for selflessness and holiness she is always mentioned.

It's inconvenient if someone robs you of a handy metaphor. If you finally printed the truth it would mean admitting that you missed it the first, second, and third time around. I've noticed a strong tendency in my profession for journalists not to like to admit that they ever missed anything or got anything wrong.

I think this is partly the reason, although in England my book got quite well reviewed because of the film, in the United States there seems to be the view that this book isn't worth reviewing. And it can't be for the usual reasons that the subject is too arcane and only of minority interest, or that there's not enough name recognition.

I believe there's also a version of multi-culturalism involved in this. That is to say, to be a Catholic in America is to be a member of two kinds of community: the communion of believers and the Catholic community, which is understood in a different sense, in other words, large numbers of Irish, Italian, Croatian, and other ethnic groups, who claim to be offended if any of the tenets of their religion are publicly questioned. Thus you are in a row with a community if you choose to question the religion. Under one interpretation of the rules of multi-culturalism that is not kosher: you can't do that because you can't offend people in their dearest identity. There are some secular people who are vulnerable to that very mistake.

I'll give you an interesting example, Walter Goodman, the *New York Times* television critic, saw my film and then wrote that he could not understand why it was not being shown on American television. He laid down a challenge to television to show this film. There was then a long silence until I got a call from Connie Chung's people in New York. They flew me up and said they would like to do a long item about the program, using excerpts from it, interviewing me and talking about the row that had resulted. They obviously wanted to put responsibility for the criticism of Mother Teresa onto me rather than adopt it themselves—they were already planning the damage control.

But they didn't make any program. And the reason they gave me was that they thought that if they did they would be accused of being Jewish and attacked in the same way as the distributors of *The Last Temptation of Christ* had been. And that this would stir up Catholic-Jewish hostility in New York. It was very honest of them to put it that way. They had already imagined what might be said and the form it might take and they had persuaded themselves that it wasn't worth it.

CHERRY: So your film has never been shown in the United States?

HITCHENS: No, and it certainly never will be. You can make that prediction with absolute certainty; and then you can brood on what that might suggest.

CHERRY: What was the response in Britain to your exposé of Mother Teresa? Did you get a lot of criticism for it?

HITCHENS: When the film was shown, it prompted the largest number of phone calls that the channel had ever logged. That was expected. It was also expected that there would be a certain amount of similarity in the calls. I've read the log, and many of the people rang to say exactly the same thing, often in the same words. I think there was an element of organization to it.

But what was more surprising was that it was also the largest number of calls in favor that the station had ever had. That's rare because it's usually the people who want to complain who lift the phone; people who liked the program don't ring up. That's a phenomenon well known in the trade, and it's a reason why people aren't actually all that impressed when the switchboard is jammed with protest calls. They know it won't be people calling in to praise and they know it's quite easy to organize.

A really remarkable number of people rung in to say it's high time there was a program like this. The logs scrupulously record the calls verbatim, and I noticed that the standard of English and of reasoning in the pro calls was just so much higher as to make one feel that perhaps all was not lost.

In addition to the initial viewer response, there was also a row in the press. But on the whole both sides of the case were put. Nonetheless, it was depressing to see how many people objected not to what was said but to its being said at all. Even among secular people there was an astonishment, as if I really had done something iconoclastic. People would say "Christopher Hitchens alleges that Mother Teresa keeps company with dictators" and so on, as though it hadn't been proven. But none of the critics have ever said, even the most hostile ones, that anything I say about her is untrue. No one has ever disproved any of that.

Probably the most intelligent review appeared in *The Tablet,* an English monthly Catholic paper. There was a long, serious and quite sympathetic review by someone who had obviously worked with the church in India and knew Mother Teresa. The reviewer said Mother Teresa's work and ideology do present some problems for the faith.

CHERRY: But in America the idea that Mother Teresa is a sacred cow who must not be criticized won out and your book and your critique of Mother Teresa never got an airing?

HITCHENS: Yes, pretty much. Everything in American reviews depends on *The New York Times Book Review.* My book was only mentioned in the batch of short notices at the end. Considering that Mother Teresa had a book out at the same time, I thought this was very strange. Any book review editor with any red corpuscles at all would put both books together, look up a reviewer with an interest in religion and ask him or her to write an essay comparing and contrasting them. I have been a reviewer and worked in a newspaper office, and that is what I would have expected to happen. That it didn't is suggestive and rather depressing.

CHERRY: The Mother Teresa myth requires the Indians to

play the role of the hapless victims. What do the Indians think of Mother Teresa and of the image she gives of India?

HITCHENS: I've got an enormous pile of coverage from India, where my book was published. And the reviews seem to be overwhelmingly favorable. Of course it comes at a time when there is a big crisis in India about fundamentalism and secularism.

There are many Indians who object to the image of their society and its people that is projected. From Mother Teresa and from her fans you would receive the impression that in Calcutta there is nothing but torpor, squalor, and misery, and people barely have the energy to brush the flies from their eyes while extending a begging bowl. Really and truly that is a slander on a fantastically interesting, brave, highly evolved, and cultured city, which has universities, film schools, theaters, book shops, literary cafes, and very vibrant politics. There is indeed a terrible problem of poverty and overcrowding, but despite that there isn't all that much mendicancy. People do not tug at your sleeve and beg. They are proud of the fact that they don't.

The sources of Calcutta's woes and miseries are the very overpopulation that the church says is no problem, and the mass influx of refugees from neighboring regions that have been devastated by religious and sectarian warfare in the name of God. So those who are believers owe Calcutta big time, they should indeed be working to alleviate what they are responsible for. But the pretense that they are doing so is a big fraud.

CHERRY: You mention in your book that Mother Teresa is used by the Religious Right and fundamentalist Protestants who traditionally are very anti-Catholic as a symbol of religious holiness with which to beat secular humanists.

HITCHENS: Yes, she's a poster girl for the right-to-life wing in America. She was used as the example of Christian idealism and family values, of all things, by Ralph Reed—the front man of the Pat Robertson forces. That's a symptom of a wider problem that I call "reverse ecumenicism," an opportunist alliance between extreme Catholics and extreme Protestants who used to exclude and anathematize one another.

In private Pat Robertson has nothing but contempt for other Christian denominations, including many other extreme Protestant ones. But in public the Christian Coalition stresses that it is very, very keen to make an alliance with Catholics. There is a shallow, opportunist ecumenicism among religious extremists, and Mother Teresa is quite willingly and happily in its service. She knows exactly who she is working for and with. But I think she is happiest when doing things like going to Ireland and intervening in the Divorce Referendum, as she did recently.

By the way, there is an interesting angle to that which has not yet appeared in print. During the Divorce Referendum the Irish Catholic church threatened to deny the sacrament to women who wanted to be remarried. There were no exceptions to be allowed: it didn't matter if you had been married to an alcoholic who beat you and sexually assaulted your children, you were not going to get a second chance in this world or the next. And that is the position that Mother Teresa intervened in Ireland to support.

Now shift the scene: Mother Teresa is a sort of confessor to Princess Diana. They have met many times. You can see the mutual interest; I'm not sure which of them needs the other the most. But Mother Teresa was interviewed by *Ladies Home Journal,* a magazine read by millions of American women, and in the course of it she says that she heard that Princess Diana was getting divorced and she really hopes so because she will be so much happier that way.

So there is forgiveness after all, but guess for whom. You couldn't have it more plain than that. I was slightly stunned myself because, although I think there are many fraudulent things about Mother Teresa, I also think there are many authentic things about her. Anyway, she was forced to issue a statement saying that marriage is God's work and can't be undone and all the usual tripe. But when she was speaking from the heart, she was more forgiving of divorce.

CHERRY: A footnote in your book criticizes Mother Teresa for forgiving you for your film about her.

HITCHENS: I said that I didn't ask for forgiveness and I wasn't aware that she could bestow it in any case. Of all the things in the book, that is the one that has attracted most hostile comment—even from friends and people who agree with me. They ask why I object to that, what's wrong with forgiveness? My explanation is that it would be O.K. if she was going to forgive everyone. When she went to Bhopal after the Union Carbide industrial accident killed thousands, she kept saying

"Forgive, forgive, forgive." It's O.K. to forgive Union Carbide for its negligence, but for a woman married to an alcoholic child abuser in Ireland who has ten children and no one to look after her, there is no forgiveness in this life or the next one. But there is forgiveness for Princess Diana.

CHERRY: There is a Roman Catholic doctrine about the redemption of the soul through suffering. This can be seen in Mother Teresa's work: she thinks suffering is good, and she doesn't use pain relievers in her clinics and so forth. Does she take the same attitude towards her own health? Does she live in accordance with what she preaches?

HITCHENS: I hesitated to cover this in my book, but I decided I had to publish that she has said that the suffering of the poor is something very beautiful and the world is being very much helped by the nobility of this example of misery and suffering.

CHERRY: A horrible thing to say.

HITCHENS: Yes, evil in fact. To say it was unchristian unfortunately would not be true, although many people don't realize that is what Christians believe. It is a positively immoral remark in my opinion, and it should be more widely known than it is.

She is old, she has had various episodes with her own health, and she checks into some of the costliest and finest clinics in the West herself. I hesitated to put that in the book because it seemed as though it would be *ad hominem* (or *ad feminam*) and I try never to do that. I think that the doctrine of hating the sin and loving the sinner is obviously a stupid one, because its a false antithesis, but a version of it is morally defensible. Certainly in arguments one is only supposed to attack the arguments and not the person presenting them. But the contrast seemed so huge in this case.

It wasn't so much that it showed that her facilities weren't any good, but it showed that they weren't medical facilities at all. There wasn't any place she runs that she could go; as far as I know, their point isn't treatment. And in fairness to her, she has never really claimed that treatment is the point. Although she does accept donations from people who have fooled themselves into thinking so, I haven't found any occasion where she has given a false impression of her work. The only way she could be said to be responsible for spreading it is that she knowingly accepts what comes due to that false impression.

CHERRY: But if people go to her clinics for the dying and they need medical care, does she send them on to the proper places?

HITCHENS: Not according to the testimony of a number of witnesses. I printed the accounts of several witnesses whose testimony I could verify and I've had many other communications from former volunteers in Calcutta and in other missions. All of them were very shocked to find when they got there that they had missed some very crucial point and that very often people who come under the false impression that they would receive medical care are either neglected or given no advice.

In other words, anyone going in the hope of alleviation of a serious medical condition has made a huge mistake. I've got so much testimony from former workers who contacted me after I wrote the book that I almost have enough material to do a sequel.

CHERRY: I have a question as one Englishman in America to another. You are a secular humanist Englishman who is a leading commentator on American culture and politics. Tell me, what is it about Americans and religion? Why is it that religion, often very primitive forms of religion, is so powerful in perhaps the richest, most advanced, most consumerist nation on Earth?

HITCHENS: I'm an atheist. I'm not neutral about religion, I'm hostile to it. I think it is a positively bad idea, not just a false one. And I mean not just organized religion, but religious belief itself.

Why is the United States so prone to any kind of superstition, not just organized religion, but cultism, astrology, millennial beliefs, UFOs, any form of superstition? I've thought a lot about it. I read Harold Bloom's book *The American Religion: The Emergence of the Post-Christian Nation* (1992) about the evolution of what he thinks of as a specifically American form of religion. There was a book by Will Herberg in the 1950s called *Protestant, Catholic, Jew* where he speculated that what was really evolving was the American way of life as a religion. And that this was a way of life that wasn't at all spiritual or intellectual but in a sense believed that all religion was valid as long as it underpinned this way of life. Somehow religion was a necessary ingredient. In other words, religion was functional. I think that's true but it's not the whole story.

Maybe—and this is a conclusion that I am reluctant to come to—it is because there is no established church here. A claim that is made for established churches is that in a way they domesticate and canalize and give a form and order to superstitious impulses. That's why they usually succeed in annexing all local cults and making them their own, etc. Part of their job is to soak up all the savagery around the place. I think from an anthropological point of view, that's partly true.

In a country that very honorably and uniquely founded itself on repudiating that idea and saying the church and the government would always be separate, and also a country that many people came to in the hope of practicing their own religion, you have both free competition and a sense of manifest destiny. I think it's out of that sort of stew that you have all these bubbles.

Chesterton used to say that, if people didn't have a belief in God, they wouldn't believe in nothing, they would believe in anything. The objection to that of course is that belief in God is believing in anything. But there's still a ghost of a point in there: if people are licensed to believe anything and call it spirituality, then they will.

CHERRY: I think maybe it's not so much not having an established church as not having a dominant church. In France you have strict separation, but the Catholic church is dominant. Yet France has very high levels of nonbelief, like countries with an established church. But in America you have free competition of churches, and lots of competing cults, and much more energy as a result.

HITCHENS: I'm not sure that people in the United States are as devout as the statistics suggest. The statistics are extraordinary if you believe them: something like 88 percent of Americans regularly attend church, and 90 percent of them believe in the devil. I would like to have a look at how the questions are formulated in these polls.

CHERRY: We have done our own polls—scientifically selected samples—in which we framed the questions ourselves, and we got very similar results to the other polls we had read. It may be that the question is not, Why do people believe this?—because perhaps they don't—but, Why do people say they believe this? There's obviously a social conditioning.

HITCHENS: Yes, that's right. People obviously feel they owe the pollsters that kind of answer.

I wonder whether the onset of the millennium is going to be as awful as I sometimes fear. There will be uneasiness among the feeble-minded and the emotionally insecure.

CHERRY: Especially in America.

HITCHENS: American fundamentalism has one huge problem which is that the United States is nowhere prefigured in the Bible. It worries them a lot, they keep trying to find it there, they try to interpret prophecies to refer to the United States, but they can't succeed—even to their own satisfaction—in getting it to come out right.

CHERRY: You have to go to the Book of Mormon?

HITCHENS: Yes, and the Seventh-Day Adventists, who descended from the Millerites. I can see that Scientology now enjoys charitable status as a religion, which I think is a real triumph. I can't get over that. You can set some idea of what it would have been like to live in third-century Nicea when Christianity was being hammered together—an experience I am very glad I did not have. Religious diversity is confused with pluralism. Because of multi-culturalism and what is called "political correctness," religion has a certain protection that it couldn't expect to have if it was a state-sponsored racket like the Church of England.

CHERRY: A lot of people who aren't religious think religion should still be beyond criticism.

HITCHENS: Certainly, because it's people's deepest and dearest beliefs, and because they are communities as well as congregations. And I suppose that in the minds of some people the feeling is "Well, you never know, it may be true and then I will go to Hell." A lot of people every now and then are visited by fear. It seems that as animals we are so constituted. At least we can know that about ourselves, but it is such a waste of the knowledge to interpret in any other way. On the other hand, I'm also impressed by the number of people who manage to get by—often without any help or support—not believing.

CHERRY: The great thing about humanism is that so many people reach the position independently, because it is not about teachers and doctrines. You just end up a humanist by following your own questions.

HITCHENS: That's true. And it doesn't have any element of wishful thinking in it, which is another advantage. Though it's the reason why I think it will always be hated but never eradicated.

CHERRY: Look at the situation in Western Europe: in Holland about 55 percent say they are humanist or non-religious; and in Britain it's up to about 30 percent and among teenagers it's 50 percent. So there's an enormous movement in Western Europe towards secularism and humanism. Yet in America it seems to be getting just more and more religious. Which, considering the convergence of culture in other areas, seems quite anomalous. Sociologists are just beginning to address this issue but haven't done so properly yet.

CHRISTOPHER HITCHENS

INTERVIEW BY SASHA ABRAMSKY
THE PROGRESSIVE
FEBRUARY 1997

Christopher Hitchens is a columnist for *The Nation* and *Vanity Fair* and a freelance contributor to numerous other publications in both Britain and the United States. He is the author of a dozen books, covering issues as diverse as Britain's plundering of the Parthenon, the conflicts in the Middle East, Anglo-American relations, and the unsaintly qualities of Mother Teresa.

An Englishman by birth and upbringing, Hitchens came to America in the early 1980s, living first in New York City and then in Washington, D.C. In 1994, I was Hitchens's intern at *The Nation*. I discovered that we both went to the same college at Oxford —Balliol—and studied the same course: Politics, Philosophy, and Economics. Now, aged forty-seven, Hitchens lives with his wife, Carol Blue, and their three-year-old daughter, Antonia, in a spacious apartment in the Adams-Morgan district of Washington, D.C.

I talked with Hitchens in his apartment. He was chain-smoking cigarettes, and we both drank generous glasses of whiskey. As with so many British journalists, Hitchens is a heavy drinker and smoker, a bon vivant with a quick tongue and an often deadly pen. At one point in the interview, "You Say You Want a Revolution" by the Beatles came on. Hitches said: "I hate this song, it's one of the few I really hate. This was the one praised by Mayor Daley as a healthy alternative to the Rolling Stones." After four hours of talking, the bottle was empty, and, as I left, Hitchens was getting ready for a late night of work.

Q: I remember reading that you grew up a navy brat.

HITCHENS: Well, I was born in 1949, in Portsmouth. It's a navy town, where all my father's ancestors seemed to come from. My father was a lifetime naval officer. The first memory I have is of Malta, which was still a British colony, technically, where my brother was born. I was brought up in a very naval, military, and conservative background. My father broke into the middle class by joining the navy. I was the first member of my family ever to go to private school or even to university. So, the armed forces had been upward mobility for him.

After the war, the general feeling was that Britain had been cheated out of its Empire. A sort of politics of resentment. It would be very common to hear people say, round about the cocktail hour, "Well, I thought *we* won the war," with rather heavy sarcasm, as the news came in that yet again Britain had to back down over Suez, or bases in Cyprus, or whatever it might be. It was a very resentful feeling that all that Churchillian rhetoric hadn't really amounted to very much in the long run. It had a powerful effect on me.

Q: What were your formative political impressions?

HITCHENS: I was precocious enough to watch the news and read the papers, and I can remember October 1956, the simultaneous crises in Hungary and Suez, very well. And getting a sense that the world was dangerous, a sense that the game was up, that The Empire was over.

I didn't form any political opinions of my own until I was a little bit older. I remember the first time I ever made a public speech, I would have been eleven or twelve. My prep school had a debate on the question of whether or not the Commonwealth Immigration Bill, which the Tories had just proposed to restrict West-Indian immigration, was justified or not. I spoke against the bill. I think I did it because nobody else would. And then, I remember deciding quite early on, having read a book by Arthur Koestler on hanging, that I was on principle opposed to capital punishment.

In 1964, when Wilson ran for Labour in October, we had a mock election in the high school. I decided I wanted the Labour Party to win, and again it wasn't very difficult to become nominated for the candidacy—because there wasn't much rivalry. We came third.

Q: Do you remember how many votes you got?

HITCHENS: No! But I remember there was a very good communist candidate that took away a lot of my constituency.

Q: Why didn't you run as a communist then?

HITCHENS: Because I was never, ever tempted by it. Maybe it was just an accident of where I was born and when. But the communists never appealed to me. And I was to a certain extent inoculated against it. I read *Darkness at Noon* before I read *The Communist Manifesto*.

No, the leftward move for me was the very rapid experience of disillusionment with the Wilson government of 1964, with the collapse of that government into the most dismal kinds of conservative orthodoxy. There was the seaman's strike of 1966 and devaluation and the sell-out of Rhodesia—a lot of stuff.

But obviously the central, defining, overarching, whatever word you want for this sort of thing, was Vietnam. The first time I went on a CND [Campaign for Nuclear Disarmament] march—Easter march as it used to be called—was in 1966, and what drew me to it principally was that CND was the main national movement making a stink about the war in Vietnam.

Q: And this is before you went to Oxford?

HITCHENS: Before I went to Oxford, which I did in late 1967.

Q: How did the Oxford culture, the college system, the tutorials, the drinking, how did all of that help mold your character?

HITCHENS: I don't think very much. I knew from some time before, having been at this rather well-placed school at Cambridge, and having done a bit of English history and economics, I knew that what I wanted to do was to read PPE [Politics, Philosophy, and Economics—a course many future journalists, diplomats, and politicians take at Oxford] at Balliol. I knew that when I was fifteen. Not only that, but I got to do it, too.

And my very first experience was one of extreme disappointment. The standard, the intellectual atmosphere, was not as rarified as everyone had led me to believe it would be. I just didn't go to classes or lectures at all.

Q: What were your politics like then?

HITCHENS: Before I went up to Oxford, I had basically been kicked out of the Labour Party—roughly the time I did go up to Oxford actually—and I associated myself there with the International Socialists. When 1968 came, I was a member of a peripheral group that had members in the single figures, which in the course of the spring and summer of 1968 ballooned into several hundred—this is just talking about in Oxford.

And one had the experience, which I've only had once in my life, and I think some people never have, of seeing what had been a minority analysis of everything, apparently confirmed by everyday newspapers. Many people were being driven to take our positions. Everything seemed to be confirmed. What we said about the Vietnam War turned out to be completely right; what we said about the emptiness of social democracy turned out to be right. What we had said about Stalinism was particularly confirmed by what happened in Poland in February and March and what happened in Czechoslovakia in August. And it was really exciting.

It was also very, very clear that the government and the authorities in general—the editor of the *Times*, even the BBC—they didn't know what was going on. And that's another feeling you don't often get.

In the summer, I went to Cuba, and we got into a huge fight with the Castro regime over a number of things: the one-party state, the maltreatment of dissenters—social and civic ones—and gay people as well. But I was there when Czechoslovakia was invaded. I was on my way to Prague on the invitation of the Czechs, to go and see Dubcek. If I'd left two days earlier I'd have got there. It's one of the biggest regrets of my life.

Q: And at that stage, if you had to identify yourself with an "ism," what would it have been?

HITCHENS: Luxemburg! Yeah, the International Socialists were often referred to as Trots, which wasn't completely right. We were Rosa Luxemburgist. Rosa Luxemburg was—still is for me—a great personal and intellectual heroine. Her analysis of Leninism and capitalism and social democracy are all worth reading right now. I wouldn't consider anyone truly politically literate if they hadn't given her work at least some study.

Q: There is a mystique that surrounds Balliol. Its students are taught to cultivate what is popularly known as "effortless superiority." You're obviously at least partially a product of this. Did it have an influence on why you chose journalism?

HITCHENS: Journalism! I'd always wanted to write and I'd always written. And by elimination—I obviously wasn't going to become a lawyer. And yes, there was something in the Balliol atmosphere conducive to this, and if I meet someone from Balliol now, yes there is a certain code that is unspoken. I neither make too much use of it, nor a fetish of it, but I don't frown on it either. This includes people who are politically opposed to me—like George Stephanopoulos: We had the same tutor, Stephen Lukes.

Q: Why did you choose to go into print journalism rather than television? I understand at one stage you were considered semiseriously for the role of the Voice of the Left on CNN's *Crossfire*.

HITCHENS: Quasi-seriously! Because it's solitary. I've always wanted to write and—it might sound pompous—I needed to write. While I was still at Oxford, I was asked by *The New Statesman*, which as then still a great magazine—*the* magazine of politics and culture in a way—to be a book reviewer, and I published my first book review in 1969. It wasn't very often that they asked me, but it was a start, and it gave me a huge advantage to be writing for them at that age.

Q: And what happened when you left Oxford?

HITCHENS: I got a scholarship [from Balliol] to travel around America. And the first thing I did when I got to New York was to go see Carey McWilliams, the great editor of *The Nation*. And he gave me people to see across America. I had to go back to England with some reluctance. I got a job on the *Times,* "Higher Education Supplement," as a social-science editor. It didn't give me much scope for writing, but I wrote book reviews for the *Times* at that stage. Then I published my first book—on Karl Marx and the Paris Commune—it was the centenary of the Commune. And *The Statesman* offered me a job on the staff, when I was twenty-two. I had realized that probably I wasn't ever going to become a novelist—it hurt—or a playwright, or anything like that.

Q: Why?

HITCHENS: Because when I was at *The Statesman*, my colleagues my age were Martin Amis, Julian Barnes, James Fenton, and Timothy Noel. And I have to say, I realized these guys were better at that kind of writing than I was. It was rather intimidating that they were so good. It made me specialize more in the generalist-type political essay. But they were very good people to work with, for style. They persuaded me it wasn't enough just to make the point; that style *was* substance, and that there was something in language itself. I learned by osmosis. These people are still my circle, my best friends.

Q: Why did you decide to come to America?

HITCHENS: The first thing I can remember I ever wanted was to go to the United States. And for reasons that are as conventional as you can imagine: I wanted to know if it was really true that it was the land of opportunity, of democracy, and individual liberty. My conclusion was that, at least as compared to the *ancien regime* under which I had been brought up, it was.

I'm a founding signatory of Charter 88 [a movement in

Britain for the creation of a written, rights-based constitutional system]. And it was very obvious to me that the whole inspiration of that movement is constitutional democracy. But all of its models, all of its actually existing inspirations were American: things like the Freedom of Information Act, however imperfect it has become, like the First Amendment, separating Church and State, guaranteeing free speech, judicial review, separation of powers, and so on—as opposed to the British system where you have traditions instead of rights.

At the same time, I've always been very keen on European unification as a means of detaching certain elements of Britain from their extreme dependence on the oligarchic part of the United States. I don't think there's any contradiction there.

Q: In your book *Blood, Class, and Nostalgia,* you write about what might be the British position within what you call "The American Imperium." As a Briton living in America, commenting on both countries, yet not quite wholly of either country, what do you think Britain's position is vis-à-vis America?

HITCHENS: What at the moment strikes me is the way American hegemony is back again in the crucial areas of politics and mass cult. I mean, to go to London now from New York or Washington—it used to be there was a lag of a few months between the conversation you'd just left in Washington and the one you were having in London. You could see that in a short while they'd be catching up with what was being talked about. Now, it's almost the same conversation: the Americanization of British politics, for example—very, very noticeable. And I don't think they're borrowing the good bits. Now they talk exactly as if they've all been schooled by Lee Atwater or Ed Rollins.

But the point about Charter 88 and my book was this: Anglophiles in the United States are defined as people who like things like the monarchy, the accent, the marmalade, the country houses, the whole *Masterpiece Theatre* conception of Britain as a theme park of feudalism and charm, whereas a pro-American in Britain tended to be someone who wanted to reassure the White House or the Pentagon that we would not desert them in their hours of need.

What I hope for, and tried to argue for in the book, is we would borrow different things and try to emulate different things. For example, the United States, instead of admiring monarchy, would be better off emulating national health, or the broadcasting standards of the BBC as it used to be. And perhaps even the tutorial system at Oxford. And the British, instead of saying we want to be the best ally, we want our chaps in Curzon Street to be the best friends of those in Langley, could be saying we'd rather borrow their Freedom of Information Act.

Q: I take it you won't be voting for Tony Blair in England this time round.

HITCHENS: I didn't vote Labour in 1979, which was the last time I could have done. But I will vote Labour in May; I would like the Labour Party to win.

Lesser evilism, incidentally, which I've spent a lifetime

opposing, is somewhat different when you're arguing about electing an opposition rather than confirming a government in place. For example, all the arguments we had against Clinton in 1992 were very cogent—and our predictions all validated, in fact we were moderate about him—but they wouldn't have translated to a vote to keep Bush as president.

No, in many ways I think that Blair is an improvement on the hypocrisy of the Labour Party. Old Labour was no fucking bargain, I can tell you that. I'm young enough to have been Old Labour and old enough to have been New Left. So it's going to take a lot to surprise me. But the word "new" has no more charms for me.

Q: One of the emerging debates is whether or not the identity politics that grew out of the New Left has a future, and whether it's capable of forming a genuine ideological and intellectual alternative to the New Right.

HITCHENS: I remember very well the first time I heard the slogan "the personal is political." I felt a deep, immediate sense of impending doom.

Q: Why?

HITCHENS: Because I was a 1968er, I really was a 1968er. And I recognized when it was over. That slogan summed it up nicely for me: "I'll have a revolution inside my own psyche." It's escapist and narcissistic. In order to take part in discussions we used to have, you were expected to have read Luxemburg, Deutsche, some Gramsci, to know the difference between Bihar and Bangladesh, to know what was meant by the Goethe Program, to understand the difference between Keynes and Schumpeter, to have read a bit of Balzac and Zola. You were expected to have broken a bit of a sweat, to have stretched your brain a bit, in order just to have a discussion.

With "the personal is political," nothing is required of you except to be able to talk about yourself, the specificity of your own oppression. That was a change of quality as well as quantity. And it fit far too easily into the consumer, me-decade, style-section, New-Age gunk.

Q: Would that hold for movements like the feminist movement after the early 1970s, the gay rights movement, maybe the environmental movement?

HITCHENS: The environmental movement at least is about something larger than itself. I mean, certainly you can't just say it's about the personal. At least there was some politics involved.

What they forgot, I think, because they all took as their model Dr. King's civil rights movement, was that the whole reason for the success of that movement was that it was not a movement for itself. The civil rights movement understood very clearly, and stated very beautifully, that it was a question of humanism, not a sectarian movement at all.

Q: What about Jesse Jackson's strategy in the early 1980s of trying to create a Rainbow Coalition? Do you think this concept is a way forward?

HITCHENS: Unfortunately, the Rainbow Coalition was an attempt to get all of these groups, all of whom wanted their own agenda, to coalesce. It was an attempt to build the same bridge but from the middle of the river. It was a sort of squaring of the circle. Let's all be a member of the coalition without giving up our individuality.

I remember countless meetings where the idea was "one more plank." And the problem is that this is what Freud called the narcissism of the small difference. People will always try to concentrate on themselves. Well, you can go to a meeting where someone says, "The meeting doesn't stop till we discuss the question not just of Cherokee lesbians, but Cherokee lesbians who have to take an outsized garment label." It's barely an exaggeration. There will always be someone who wants it all to be about them. So what was for a moment something that was social, general, collective, education, and a matter of solidarity, can be very quickly dissolved into petty factionalism. Therefore, coalition-building is reassembling something out of fragments that needn't be fragmented in the first place.

Q: In your writing, you reserve a special hatred for Clinton. What is it in particular about Clinton that you hate so much?

HITCHENS: It goes back to what I said about Wilson in a way. Clinton comes on as someone who is definitely modern, no question about that, very much at home with modernity. Wilson's "white heat of technology" was a very clever means of talking revolution while in fact making sordid bargains.

It's nothing to me if there's a moderate, corrupt Republican about the place, really. That's part of the wallpaper of living in a consumer society, and the damage they do is mainly to their own side. But if there's someone who's appealing to the idealism of the young and the visions of the left and getting away with it by doing that, then he's trampling on territory that I care about. It's like in a labor dispute, people dislike the scab much more than they do the boss. And there's something completely cowardly and shabby—and ingratiating—about Clinton's personality as well that I find repulsive.

Q: Do you see a viable alternative emerging?

HITCHENS: I think we're in for a very long period of conservative rule. It depends how long term you're prepared to think. But we're living in one of those periods where, on the world stage, only capitalism is revolutionary, not just in rich countries, but also in poor ones and also in countries that used to be state-capitalist. This is a situation that wouldn't have been at all unfamiliar to the founders of the socialist movement. It would have been exactly true in the nineteenth century.

On NAFTA, free trade is going to go on. I don't think we should waste our time. But it has many of the problems of the first industrial revolution. It's extremely undemocratic: it's very unstable and very promiscuous.

Q: You're very much an internationalist.

HITCHENS: I take capitalism very seriously, always have. It has, in fact, survived its crises—at huge fucking cost, let's not forget: war, empire. But still, it has survived. But it has not outlived its contradictions. If the world is one economy, why not make it one society? I look forward to the argument on this one. What I won't do is spend ten seconds on the argument as to whether a plant should be in Michigan or Ontario, or for that matter in California or Tijuana.

Q: A lot would disagree with you on this.

HITCHENS: They believe they can build a politics of populism against this. I'm not going to help them. They just will find out they can't build a politics against this. What we really need is a new Internationale—and that's a heavy responsibility. Sounds very utopian at the moment.

Q: What about your support for some recent international interventions, such as the one in Haiti?

HITCHENS: It was very important to remind people that the U.S. military plays far too great a role in defining policy. This is something very few people would say. Why were the right and the generals and the CIA so hostile to doing anything about it? That was very important to me, the military subversion of the Clinton Administration—annexation really, because he was very ready to do nothing. It was part of the battle to prevent the banana-ization of things. They were protecting their friends, the Haitian junta.

It goes back to the arguments of the 1930s that Europe was none of their business and they were going to build a New Deal paradise at home, so who gave a shit about triumphing over fascism? Why don't we simply demand the government acts according to its proclaimed principles? People like Noam [Chomsky] and others, who were visibly uneasy about Bosnia, I think had the difficulty of using any argument that suggests the American government can be a moral agent.

Q: What do you say about that?

HITCHENS: You could say the same about any government. Why was the right against doing anything about Bosnia? The only ones who said any differently were the neo-cons, and for them the alarm-bell word was "genocide." Left and liberal people were saying, "Well, we don't want another quagmire like Vietnam."

But the argument against Vietnam was not that an innocent, naïve America had been suckered into Vietnam, for heaven's sake! That's an affront to the anti-war movement, and I wasn't going to have anything to do with that! The collapse of Yugoslavia into the hands of ethnic fascists could have been avoided or impeded if there'd been an intervention earlier than there was.

Q: Moving on to perhaps the subject that got you into hottest water with the left: abortion. Could you talk a little about your view on this?

HITCHENS: Two points I wanted to make. One, that the term "unborn child" has been made a propaganda phrase by the people who called themselves "pro-life." But it's something that has moral and scientific realities. It's become very evident indeed that this is not just a growth upon the mother.

If that's true, what are the problems? It need not qualify the woman's right to choose. It need not. But it would be a very bold person to say that what was being chosen didn't come up. What I argued in my column was this was a social phenomenon. This is the next generation we're talking about. Considering the unborn as candidate members—potential members—of the next generation; wouldn't that strengthen the argument for socialized medicine, child care, prenatal care?

There's a reason why this is the only country where it's a mania. Because it's between the fundamentalists and the possessive individualists. It's ruined politics, absorbed a huge amount of energy that should have been spent elsewhere.

Q: But you're not agreeing with the religious right on this one?

HITCHENS: No one who is not for the provision of sex education, contraception, and child care should be allowed to have any position on abortion at all—and those who do should be met with fusillades. Women will decide it, that's a matter of fact, as much as a principle.

Q: So, what is your position regarding the continued legal status of abortion?

HITCHENS: There's no choice but choice. I mean that to sound the way it does sound. But there are choices about the conditions in which that choice is made.

I'm very much opposed to euthanasia. I've never understood why more of these people can't commit suicide. Why do they need a Dr. Kevorkian? It's very theatrical. I believe in a right to decide.

But I'm against all blurrings. There's a very sharp dividing line in the case of an infant. I'm against fooling with that. Everything in me rebels against that. The conclusion I've come to as to why it's such a toxic question in America is it isn't about the rights of the unborn child. I think it's an argument about patriarchy. It is a metaphor for the status of women in what is still in some ways a frontier society.

Q: Give me a few choice encounters with famous people you've met.

HITCHENS: Most of them are disappointments. Claude Cockburn once said that it's awful how things often turn out exactly the way they're supposed to be. Some things are what they're cracked up to be.

So when I met Nelson Mandela he was unbelievably charming and graceful and courteous and self-effacing: just like he was supposed to be. It was a bit of a letdown.

We met Vaclav Havel last month: rumpled, chain-smoking, and democratic. What was the point of doing that?

Thatcher was a sadomasochistic person with no self-doubt.

Hillary was full of self-pity and self-righteousness.

Let's see who else we've got here. Abu Nidal offered to use me as someone to transmit a death threat to another Palestinian. Which he later carried out. Which I also delivered! These are all politicians, of course.

Andreas Papandreou was extremely rhetorical and bombastic.

Gerry Adams was very sentimental.

Willie Brandt probably.

Q: Why?

HITCHENS: There was a meeting in Washington where everyone had come to accuse him of selling out to the West for having doubts about cruise missiles, and all that. "How dare Germany not be belligerent?" being the line of the day! And I said I had come to ask him what it was like being with George Orwell in Barcelona as volunteers fighting against fascism. He welcomed the change of subject.

[*Hitchens's wife, Carol Blue, intervenes:* "What about the crazy Kurd with the eagle?"]

No one's ever heard of him. Abdullah Ocalan, leader of the PKK. Wore a Stalin mustache and had a large eagle—live eagle—tethered to his desk. I think to create some kind of impression—of destiny. He also brushed his hair like Stalin.

Clinton turned his back on me when I asked him about the execution of Rickey Ray Rector, even though he'd been hoping for a change of subject from the press conference about Gennifer Flowers.

John Major was an ingratiating, amiable mediocrity.

Barry Goldwater was a man of staunch but limited principle—who said that his dearest wish was to give Jerry Falwell a kick in the ass!

General Videla of Argentina wouldn't let me go till he'd confessed to a few murders, eagerly confessed to a few murders.

Nor would Roberto D'Aubuisson of El Salvador. In other words, with them you don't get anything but a pig with a grunt.

Q: What about Auden? You mention him a lot.

HITCHENS: Never met him. I heard him read. Met Isherwood and met Spender, but I never met Auden. I heard him read at Cambridge. I remember the poem he read: It was called "On the Circuit." Which ends, "God bless the USA/So large/So friendly/And so rich." Yes, he keeps coming up. It's amazing how he does. I'd love to have met him, but I can't start on people I wish I'd met. It would go on too long.

HITCHENS
ON LITERATURE

INTERVIEW BY J. C. GABEL AND JAMES HUGHES
STOP SMILING, ISSUE 20: BOXING
APRIL 2005

STOP SMILING: You've written on a number of occasions, but never explained entirely, that you write in a somewhat post-humous manner.

HITCHENS: Yes. Write as if it's your last words. Because then you can be sure that you don't wonder, "Will the agent like this? Will my publisher say, 'Well, couldn't we punch it up a bit more or make it more fancy?' What will my family think?" All the things that constrain people.

STOP SMILING: Does that work as a deterrent to you being edited?

HITCHENS: Yes. It does, I think. Because people would judge you a lot more if they think, "Well, he won't do [this or that]." They'll say, "Don't use the word *Promethean*." Actually, that happened recently. I used the word *Promethean* and the editors said, "Take that out because people won't know what *Promethean* means." I said, "Maybe they won't. I'll cut it out if you give me another synonym for it. You give the words that would stand in for it and I'll change it." "There doesn't seem to be one," they said. "No, there isn't, is there?" You either know what *Promethean* means or you don't. If you do, it saves you about 50 words. And if you don't, then you can look it up! So I said, "No. I'm going to keep it, because it's an important word and it's actually not condescending to Americans in the least. You have to condescend far more by finding the 50-word substitute. No, I won't change it. Fuck you. And I don't mean to publish in your magazine, either, for that matter."

I'm reading this review, and I happen to remember—I forget what the review was of—but they mentioned Tolstoy. This sentence said, "This is reminiscent of the 19th-century Russian novelist Count Leo Tolstoy." Now, clearly, the author [of the review] had not written this. But someone had thought, "Not all our readers know who Tolstoy is. We better tell them." This is ridiculous! If you don't know who he is, that doesn't tell you any more than what you don't know.

STOP SMILING: Same as "Homer of *The Iliad*."

HITCHENS: Yes. "Homer's *Iliad*, based on Homer's *The Iliad*." "The 19th-century Russian novelist . . ." People would flock to Tolstoy and say, "Who's that?" They know no more if you just said that. It's insulting, the people who do that. It broke completely the rhythm of the guy's sentence. Whatever he had, it's completely undone by shoving all this crap in. It's yet another case of you thinking, "What are they taking me for? Do they think I'm a moron?"

STOP SMILING: It's insulting.

HITCHENS: There's those who don't know Tolstoy and those who do. It isn't helping those who don't. I understand helping those who don't: I try not to use a foreign phrase if it isn't dead obvious in the context.

STOP SMILING: You didn't happen to read Kurt Vonnegut's piece "Cold Turkey" for *In These Times* a while back?

HITCHENS: No. I usually would read anything he wrote, I guess. Though he's running on empty now.

STOP SMILING: He is. But he apparently still smokes two packs of unfiltered Pall Malls a day.

HITCHENS: He wrote one of the best pieces on giving up smoking I've ever read.

STOP SMILING: Did he give it up?

HITCHENS: He gave it up, and then he said he noticed he got a bit fatter. He's a very [tall] guy to begin with. I don't know— he's well over six feet. But he noticed that he'd ballooned out. He felt so proud and noble having given this up, and waking up feeling so happy. Until every member of his family came to him and begged him to start smoking again, because he was unbearable. Un-*fucking* bearable.

I've always liked Vonnegut's stuff. I met him, too. We did an event once in L.A. He can be great fun. He is a wonderful manic-depressive. He's very funny about being mad and miserable. And I've liked almost everything I've read by him. But I don't think I'll reread it now, and I really doubt I'll read it again. Timing is good. *[Quoting*

Vonnegut] "If there's one thing, you're a waste of common sense." "The unexamined life is not worth living. Okay. What if the examined life turns out to be a clunker?" It's a good quote. The placing of *clunker* in that sentence is fucking good. When he talked about how he used to work for General Electric, he said, "This is the time when Ronald Reagan was General Electric's traveling spokesman, warning the whole of America against socialism. Mr. Reagan and I never met, so I remained a socialist." Good throwaway stuff. And especially *Slaughterhouse-Five.* The book will survive. The fact that he should be there, and the best book on the issue should be written by a German-American, is a wonderful factor.

Vonnegut is absolutely—he's like E. L. Doctorow. He's an actually paid-up member of the Democratic Socialists of America. He could never surprise you politically in a million years.

STOP SMILING: Are there any contemporary fiction writers you read?

HITCHENS: Yes, to the ruin of my life.

STOP SMILING: Do you like Milan Kundera?

HITCHENS: I like Kundera. He hasn't written much lately, but I enjoy him very much. His essays are very good, too.

STOP SMILING: He still hasn't been back to [the] Czech Republic, has he?

HITCHENS: He could never get himself around much over there.

STOP SMILING: Even after *The Unbearable Lightness of Being*?

HITCHENS: No, no, he couldn't do it. He was ashamed of having left and not having stuck around with the literary people who endured it all and then defeated it. And also he used to be pessimistic. I quarreled with him about that.

STOP SMILING: In print?

HITCHENS: I wrote an attack on him in '88, just before the end of Communism. It was in *The Nation*. I did this thing on the anniversary of the invasion of Prague. It had been 20 years since the occupation. I said I thought that the whole system was going to collapse. I did actually say that. Some people like Solzhenitsyn [in Russia], Kolakowski in Poland, and Kundera write about Soviet Communism as if it was unbelievably frightening, total, organized, menacing. It gratifies something in themselves to say, "This is an enemy that can't bend, can't reform, etc." It was a mistake. Essentially, it was boring and useless, and it's going to collapse. They had much better chances of living under it now. And I was right about it. I was correct and they were wrong. People started to give an excuse for staying in Prague: "It's hopeless. You can't do anything. You've got to leave and go live in Paris. Those who stayed behind and published samizdats from the underground, they're wasting their time being silly." It's a shame. Have you ever read Peter Schneider's novels?

STOP SMILING: No. Is he German?

HITCHENS: Yes. Actually, he's from a remote province of Germany, but for most of his life he's been a Berliner, which is a special kind of German to be, I think. He wrote a cycle of three novels about Berlin. They're all brilliant. All the girls get pregnant in them. Anyway, he's a great guy. He's still a good friend of mine. He's written fantastically good essays about going over the Wall, and he came across a story a few years ago which he thought would be a wonderful account to write.

Towards the end of the war, in Germany, the Nuremberg laws had not rounded up yet all of those who were German Aryan that had been married to Jews. They had still found husbands and wives who—the Nurembergers were completely clear whether you could be murdered for marrying them. In Berlin, there were quite a few of these—some hundreds of them. But [the Nazis] were catching up to it. They were saying, "Okay, maybe we should finish these people off." These few hundred men and women found help from other families. "You can move into Uncle Freddie's fun dacha, or you can [get a fake Russian ID]. They won't find you. They're too busy now. It won't be long now before it's over. We'll help you out."

Several thousand Berliners did at least something for them: a bed for the night, a ration book, help, lying to the cop when he comes to the door. Saying, "No, we don't have anyone staying here." Not much. But all they could do to survive. Everyone's always looking for stories about good Germans. Germans are looking for [such stories]. [Schneider] came across all the documents about this operation. He wrote a piece about it for [*The*] *New York Times Magazine*. Very good piece. Everybody hated it.

STOP SMILING: Why did they hate it?

HITCHENS: Because it disproved the excuse that there's nothing you can do. Schneider said, "I should have seen that coming." They *hated* it! Everyone's reason was, "We would have loved to. I had so many Jewish friends. I would have helped them. But you know, you've no idea, Herr Hitchens, the terror—the nightmare—we lived through. No one could do anything."

"Oh, yes, you could. Except *you fucking didn't do even a tiny thing*. You wouldn't even give a neighbor a bed for the night, you asshole."

Now that is—if you understand the story—a very profound story about human issues that are just as true in Iraq—everyone knows that they were cowards and scum. No one now has the chance to regret. And they take it in the most horrible way. *[Adopting an Iraqi accent]* "I pay my respects to citizens of U.S."—yeah, fuck you! I saw you last year, shouting, "We give our blood to Saddam!" Come on! Who are you fooling? Michael Moore?

STOP SMILING: Getting back to authors: I had read recently that Kissinger persuaded Alexander Solzhenitsyn to not speak at the White House.

HITCHENS: No.

STOP SMILING: Could you tell us what that story was about?

HITCHENS: When Solzhenitsyn was kicked out of the Soviet Union, it was an amazing thing, because they were admitting that there was nothing they could do about the guy. This single guy had written a history [of Russia post-Revolution], privately. They defamed him in every possible way. They denounced him on television. There was nothing he could do to get by. And [the Soviets] finally decided that, we have to throw him out. The USSR cannot live with him within [its borders]. When he was picked up, people thought [he was going to jail]. But he was taken to the airport and dropped in Switzerland.

Already it was a fantastic story: they can't have one such person in their borders. You knew. So he decided he wants to live in America. He comes to the United States in '75, '76. Nixon's gone; Ford is president. There is a huge amount of pressure from American authors and human rights groups to petition [on Solzhenitsyn's behalf]. "This guy's a hero of the Cold War. He should be invited back to the White House. He should be given a medal. He should at least be given a decent dinner." Kissinger told Ford, "No, Mr. President, we shouldn't have this man. He's too dangerous. It will upset my negotiations with Brezhnev."

The only thing Ford will be remembered for aside from the Nixon pardon is that he missed the chance to have Solzhenitsyn to dinner—on Kissinger's advice. The other thing he should be remembered for is giving the green light for the invasion of East Timor. Now, no one's remembered enough for that. But that's it. That's the whole Ford story. He told Solzhenitsyn to fuck off and invaded East Timor. A great president. A great American.

Now, Solzhenitsyn is dumped in Geneva. He's told that Vladimir Nabokov lives here. He called Nabokov and asked if he could come and see him. Nabokov said sure. He was living in Montreux at the time. I collect meetings that never occurred, but should have. Orwell wanted to meet Camus in Paris. Orwell made the appointment—the Commie never showed up—and off he fucked. Solzhenitsyn went to [Nabokov's] hotel in Montreux. He was so intimidated—it was quite a grand hotel, and he didn't have much to wear—he couldn't face going in. Nabokov never forgave people who made fun of him if they didn't show up for appointments. When Solzhenitsyn summoned the nerve to call up again, Nabokov said, "Actually, I don't think so. In any case, I'll ask you not to interrupt my translation of *Eugene Onegin*." Such a pity.

STOP SMILING: There's probably a book in there somewhere.

HITCHENS: "Missed Meetings." There's another one—oh fuck, what is it? It'll come to me. Anyway, I used to think I might like to write fiction or poetry. Which, the truth of the matter is, I can't really. I mean, I can. I could if my children's lives weren't at stake. "Will you write a short story, or will you see them roasted?" "Okay." I like short fiction. Or a sonnet. I was very lucky in knowing someone like Ian McEwan, Martin Amis, Julian Barnes. I realized from hanging out with them, "You're bad." I'll leave that bit to them. I might do something with the essay, but I'm not going near them. I think they're very good.

I'm reading this guy Orhan Pamuk, if you know him. Turkish writer. He's a very brilliant Turkish novelist who, I think, is onto something. You'll be hearing about him. And I read George Eliot a lot, whenever I can. And Joyce and Borges. None of them contemporaries. But they really are contemporary. It's the gold standard, the stuff people will always read.

STOP SMILING: If you could meet one dead author, who would it be?

HITCHENS: George Eliot. Eliot or Nabokov. I'd rather have met Orwell, I think. He was the guy who seemed to come the nearest to making journalism into literature, which is what I'm trying to do.

HITCHENS ON THE WARS IN IRAQ AND AFGHANISTAN

INTERVIEW BY JON STEWART
THE DAILY SHOW WITH JON STEWART
AUGUST 25, 2005

STEWART: Hey, welcome back! A contributing editor to *Vanity Fair* and an author, his latest book is *Thomas Jefferson: Author of America*. Please welcome back to the program Christopher Hitchens. Christopher!

[Hitchens enters]

Come on.

HITCHENS: Don't get up. No please don't get up.

STEWART: You sir, a pleasure.

[They shake hands and both gesture to the chairs]

No you, you! Good to see you.

HITCHENS: Nice to be back.

STEWART: Welcome to the show.

HITCHENS: It's very nice for you to have me back.

STEWART: The book is *Thomas Jefferson: Author of America.*

We are going to talk about that in a little bit. But I'm going to tell you about why you're here. You're here to help me. Christopher Hitchens you are one of the only men to travel, maybe the only man to travel to all three Axis of Evil countries.

[Audience laughs]

HITCHENS: Yes that's true.

STEWART: That is correct.

HITCHENS: I think I'm the only one to have written from there. There may have been a diplomat who's been there, there's certainly an arms dealer or two. But I have—

[Audience laughs]

STEWART: Good company.

HITCHENS: —been to North Korea and Iran and Iraq, several times, and in Afghanistan, and on the Pakistan border.

STEWART: Okay, so there's a Eurail pass that many people don't get punched.

HITCHENS: Well the frequent flyers stuff in Afghan Airlines, you don't wanna know.

STEWART: No, it's a little rough. It ain't a bag of peanuts, I'm sure. Here's what I wanna ask you, here's how you're going to help me. Help me understand why I am wrong about Iraq. I am confused; I don't know what stay—

HITCHENS: I can see that—

STEWART: I don't know what stay—

HITCHENS: —I just watched your act.

STEWART: I know. I don't know what staying the course means.

HITCHENS: I can see that too.

STEWART: I don't know what, when he says this, "We're going to fight 'em over there, instead of fighting 'em over here." I think, "Those other dudes who just had planes were just twenty of them. It's not a nation that attacked us, it was an ideology." Explain to me why I'm wrong.

HITCHENS: Well, I'll give you something.

STEWART: Please.

HITCHENS: Just uh, saying fighting them over there instead of over here is contradicting himself. It's either global or it isn't. So we're either fighting them everywhere or nowhere.

You make yourself a hostage to fortune. The next bomb that goes off in London, people say, "I thought we'd taken care of that by fighting them there." That, that's stupid.

[Audience laughs]

And that's his bid for, um, *[indecipherable]*.

STEWART: Here is what I don't understand. Out of Pakistan, Saudi Arabia, and Iran are the two greatest supporters of terrorism in that region. North Korea, uh, and Iran, and Pakistan are the greatest threats in terms of weapons of mass destruction and proliferation. Uh, why then the urgency to go into Iraq, other than as an experiment drawn up on a bulletin board that would create a flowering of democracy—

HITCHENS: No.

STEWART: —that would change a region overnight—

HITCHENS: Well, the last—

STEWART: —to suddenly love and respect us.

HITCHENS: Okay. I guess everyone's entitled to one softball question. Now, you just did give me one.

STEWART: Really?

HITCHENS: Urgency, the big argument is, "Were we right to confirm Saddam Husain in power, after defeating him in Kuwait? Should he be left in power in 1991?" My side says no, that's the original mistake—

STEWART: And Bush's dad said yes.

HITCHENS: And Bush's dad said yes, and it is very good that his son has cancelled that mistake. To say it's urgent, having let Iraq rot and crash for nearly twelve years, thirteen years, that's not urgency. Second thing is, there are four conditions under which a country can say its, can be said—told—its sovereignty is over. Um, one is repeated aggression against neighboring states, one is fooling around with a non-proliferation treaty, one is harboring gangsters and internationally wanted terrorists, and one is genocide. Which if you sign the convention it means you have to act, you're mandated to prevent or punish. Iraq had broken all four, more than once. And the United States said if it passed legislation in 1998 unanimously, 98 to nothing, the Iraq Liberation Act, it shall be the policy of the United States to remove this regime and begin the Middle East again. What's wrong with that? Anyone who wanted to complain should have written to their Democratic senator in '98 and said, "What's this about you promising to remove Saddam?"

STEWART: Here's why—

HITCHENS: And they didn't—

STEWART: Here's why we didn't write.

HITCHENS: —because it was an obviously right thing to be wanting to do.

STEWART: No, because it was an obviously symbolic thing to do, and nobody here thought anybody would be crazy enough—

HITCHENS: No, no, no.

STEWART: —to get into the British and Churchillian method of, "Hey let's just go into the Mid-East and redraw the map the way we think it should be drawn—"

HITCHENS: We're not redrawing the map.

STEWART: —What could happen there?"

HITCHENS: We're not redrawing the map.

[Audience applauds]

STEWART: We're not redrawing the map?

HITCHENS: No. The, excuse me . . . ahh the applause is dying faintly away.

[Audience laughs]

I might get a clap before I'm done.

[Audience applauds]

Thank you.

STEWART: People very much appreciate it. By the way, I really enjoy this—

HITCHENS: Um, now I've lost my place.

STEWART: Oh, I'm sorry.

[Audience laughs]

HITCHENS: I really can't remember where we were just before that. This is terrible.

STEWART: You were saying to me that you agree that Bush is, uh, conducting this incompetently.

[Audience laughs]

HITCHENS: Yes. I have just—

STEWART: The old Bugs Bunny trick.

HITCHENS: —I have just written a long article for *The Weekly Standard*, which will say exactly, does say, exactly that.

STEWART: Is that true?

HITCHENS: Yeah.

STEWART: So—

HITCHENS: But I think he's right on the main principle.

STEWART: So let me try and get your position then, and it may be one that is not as far from me as perhaps I thought.

HITCHENS: Unfortunately, you go to war with the president you have.

[Audience laughs]

STEWART: *[laughing]* That is a really frightening proposition.

HITCHENS: He's right on the main point. We have deadly enemies—we're in front of them, we cannot retreat. They do mean us harm and, uh, it is wrong to say that the cause of terrorism is our resistance to it, which is the root fallacy that's now being put around.

STEWART: Here's—

HITCHENS: To say if we weren't mean to them, they wouldn't be so mean to us—

STEWART: Here's, here's where I can see the difference.

HITCHENS: —Absolute bullshit.

STEWART: I agree with, uh, all your premises. I disagree that going into Iraq was the way to clarify those. I guess what I'm saying is, I agree that there are people out there who want to do harm to us. What was the other one?

[Audience laughs]

HITCHENS: Wait, oh no I remember now—

STEWART: Why is this night different from all other nights?

[Audience laughs]

HITCHENS: To say the Iraq Liberation Act was bluffing . . . Oh I've got it now—

STEWART: Alright.

HITCHENS: —I've got it now. No we're not trying to redraw the map, the Bin Laden-ists are trying to redraw the map. They don't think Iraq should exist. They don't recognize the borders of Iraq, Lebanon, Jordan, Palestine—

STEWART: But Iraq is, I mean—

HITCHENS: —They think it should all be part of—

STEWART: But let's face the facts—

HITCHENS: —a huge Islamic caliphate empire.

STEWART: But Iraq is, I mean –

HITCHENS: They're the ones who want to redraw the map.

STEWART: But let's go back to the other thing, because we're on to something—

HITCHENS: We're saying we will save Iraq and make it a federal democracy.

STEWART: We, we . . . we're coming to common ground. There are people out there who want to hurt us—

HITCHENS: Yeah that was a bit platitude-ist of me, I must say.

STEWART: Yeah, uh. There's evil in the world—

HITCHENS: Next I'll be saying the world is a dangerous place.

STEWART: —Yeah, exactly.

[Audience laughs]

HITCHENS: Well, you trip me up.

STEWART: And to resist terrorism is . . .

HITCHENS: Oh, the big fallacy is the people who say, "There wouldn't be all these terrorists in Iraq if we hadn't gone there." That, that's capitulation. I mean, Zarqawi was there before we got there. Uh, Mr. Yasin, who blew up the World Trade Center, was being sheltered there since 1993. And if you want to see the Iraq—

STEWART: Find me a country in the Middle East that you can't name five guys who tried to blow something up in the United States.

[Audience laughs]

HITCHENS: These are the guys—

STEWART: Pick one.

[Audience applauds]

I'll give you five in Qatar, I'll give you a couple who are probably working for us right now.

[Audience laughs]

HITCHENS: You name, you name me, okay, but you name me the one where it's now believed by most liberals that there is no problem of that kind, that there was no Saddam-terror connection. That's what I'm arguing about.

STEWART: That there was a Saddam—

HITCHENS: The guy who has hijacked the *Achille Lauro*, wheeled Mr. Klinghoffer's chair off the side of the boat, was also found hiding in Baghdad. I went to see Abu Nidal—

STEWART: But that is the old school . . . but that is the old school terrorism and you know it. There is a different—

HITCHENS: Zarqawi is the most dangerous man in Afghanistan, possibly more than Bin Laden. Certainly, the second dangerous, most second dangerous. In Iraq before we got there. The people who say that the violence of these people is our fault are masochistic and capitulation-ist, and they should not be—they should be ignored—

STEWART: But the people who are saying that we shouldn't fight in Iraq aren't saying it's our fault. That is the conflation that is most disturbing to me. That dissent—

HITCHENS: Don't you hear people say that we made them nasty and mean?

STEWART: I hear people say a lot of stupid shit.

[Audience laughs]

HITCHENS: Okay.

STEWART: But, what I'm saying is—

HITCHENS: You'll promise me you'll never say that?

STEWART: —there is reasonable dissent in this country about the way this war has been conducted that has nothing to do with people believing we should cut and run from the terrorists or we should show weakness in the face of terrorism—

HITCHENS: Alright.

STEWART: —or that we believe that, uh, we have in some way brought this upon ourselves. They believe this war is being conducted without transparency, without credibility, and without competence.

HITCHENS: I'm sorry, sunshine. I just watched you ridicule the president for saying that he wouldn't give a—

STEWART: No, you misunderstood why. That is not why—

HITCHENS: —a timetable. And you said . . .

STEWART: —That is not why I ridiculed the president. Why I ridiculed the president was he refuses to answer questions from adults as though we were adults, and falls back upon platitudes and phrases and talking points that does a disservice to the goals that he himself shares with the very people he needs to convince.

HITCHENS: You want me to believe that you're dying to be on his side?

[Audience applauds]

There they go. They did it again.

[Hitchens motions to the audience and pounds on the table. Stewart playfully grasps Hitchens by the head]

Come on, come on *[indecipherable]*.

[Stewart props up Thomas Jefferson: Author of America*]*

You want . . . you want me to believe that really you're secretly on his side, you just wish he was more persuasive? You want me to believe that?

STEWART: I secretly need him to be on my side.

HITCHENS: Okay.

STEWART: He's too important and powerful a man not to be.

HITCHENS: Do you want to do Jefferson's dick at all? *[Hitchens gestures to his book]*

STEWART: You want to do Jefferson's dick right now?

HITCHENS: Well, I thought we might.

STEWART: Alright, the book is *Thomas Jefferson,* it's on the bookshelves now.

[Audience laughs]

And it has a lot of relevance to our discussion now.

HITCHENS: Yes.

[Audience laughs]

STEWART: Tell me, tell me what it is. What's the discussion and then we'll go, because we're going to have to edit the whole crazy thing—

HITCHENS: There are two things. One, it's a book about the Founding Fathers as if they had penises. Most founding father books omit the dick. I put it in.

[Audience and Stewart laugh]

The other is people ask me, as I'm sure they ask you, um, "What would Jefferson think? Did he believe that, uh, American democracy should be exported?" And I say yes. And there is a very important chapter in the book about how he decides to go to war, unilaterally, with the Islamic terrorist states in North Africa, sometimes known as the Barbary States. Without consulting Congress.

STEWART: Can I say this? Can I say this—

HITCHENS: Mm-hmm.

STEWART: —without even reading the book? Bush is Jefferson.

HITCHENS: Yeah. Hold that thought ladies and gentlemen.

[Stewart laughs]

STEWART: And may I, may I do this? Because you asked for it and you deserved it and you earned it. A round of applause for Christopher Hitchens.

HITCHENS: Oh please.

[Audience applauds]

I'm going, I'm done now.

[Stewart playfully grabs Hitchens arm]

STEWART: Christopher Hitchens! We'll be right back.

HITCHENS: It's been real.

[Hitchens and Stewart shake hands and speak off mic]

QUESTIONS OF FAITH

IN CONVERSATION WITH MARILYN SEWELL
INTERVIEW BY RANDY GRAGG
PORTLAND MONTHLY
JANUARY 2010

Christopher Hitchens's 2007 book *God Is Not Great: How Religion Poisons Everything* has made him arguably the nation's most notorious atheist. Already renowned as a political columnist for *Vanity Fair, Slate*, and other magazines and known for his frequent punditry on the political TV circuit, Hitchens's barbed manifesto against religion has earned him debates across the country, often with the very fundamentalist believers his book attacks.

But as a precursor to his upcoming January 5 appearance at the Arlene Schnitzer Concert Hall, *Portland Monthly* invited Hitchens to an encounter more befitting the Rose City: a conversation with a liberal believer—Marilyn Sewell, the recently retired minister of the First Unitarian Church of Portland. A former teacher and psychotherapist and the author of numerous books, Sewell, over seventeen years, grew Portland's downtown Unitarian congregation into one of the largest in the United States.

—Randy Gragg, former editor-in-chief of *Portland Monthly*

SEWELL: Your book, *God Is Not Great* is a sweeping indictment of how religion perpetuates war, exploitation, and oppression throughout history. What inspired you to turn from critiquing politics to critiquing religion?

HITCHENS: My political life has been informed by the view that if there was any truth to religion there wouldn't really be any need for politics. A crucial element in the way I write, as well as what I write about, has been informed by my atheism. Why this book at this time? By the early part of this century I became convinced that religion was back in a big way with the Parties of God—as they dare call themselves—not just in Iran and among Al-Qaeda and Hezbollah, but with Messianic Jewish settlers trying to steal other people's land in the name of God to try and bring on Armageddon with help from Christian forces in the United States. These forces overlap with the same Christians who want pseudo-science taught to American children with taxpayers' money and with the Vatican saying that, "Well AIDS in Africa may be bad, but condoms would be worse." I thought that the moment—with a capital M—had arrived when enough people might be willing to fight back. And I and others—Richard Dawkins, Daniel Dennett, and Sam Harris—all came to the same conclusion independently. Let's not boast, but it seems we weren't completely wrong.

SEWELL: In the book you write that, at age nine, you experienced the ignorance of your scripture teacher Mrs. Watts and then later, at twelve, your headmaster tried to justify religion as a comfort when facing death. It seems you were an intuitive atheist. But did you ever try religion again?

HITCHENS: I belong to what is a significant minority of human beings: Those who are—as Pascal puts it in his *Pensées*, his great apology for Christianity—"so made that they cannot believe." As many as 10 percent of us just never can bring themselves to take religion seriously. And since people often defend religion as natural to humans (which I wouldn't say it wasn't, by the way), the corollary holds too: there must be respect for those who simply can't bring themselves to find meaning in phrases like "the Holy Spirit."

SEWELL: Well, could it be that some people are "so made" for faith, and you are so made for the intellectual life?

HITCHENS: I don't have whatever it takes to say things like "the grace of God." All that's white noise to me, not because I'm an intellectual. For many people, it's gibberish. Likewise, the idea that the Koran was dictated by an archaic illiterate is a fantasy. As so far the most highly evolved of the primates, we do seem in the majority to have a tendency to worship, and to look for patterns that lead to supernatural conclusions. Whereas, I think that there is no supernatural dimension whatever. The natural world is quite wonderful enough. The more we know about it, the much more wonderful it is than any supernatural proposition.

SEWELL: The religion you cite in your book is generally the fundamentalist faith of various kinds. I'm a liberal Christian, and I don't take the stories from the scripture literally. I don't believe in the doctrine of atonement (that Jesus died for our sins, for example). Do you make any distinction between fundamentalist faith and liberal religion?

HITCHENS: I would say that if you don't believe that Jesus of Nazareth was the Christ and Messiah, and that he rose again from the dead and by his sacrifice our sins are forgiven, you're really not in any meaningful sense a Christian.

SEWELL: Let me go someplace else. When I was in seminary I was particularly drawn to the work of theologian Paul Tillich. He shocked people by describing the traditional God—as *you* might as a matter of fact—as, "an invincible tyrant." For Tillich, God is "the ground of being." It's his response to, say, Freud's belief that religion is mere wish fulfillment and comes from humans' fear of death. What do you think of Tillich's concept of God?"

HITCHENS: I would classify that under the heading of "statements that have no meaning—at all." Christianity, remember, is really founded by St. Paul, not by Jesus. Paul says, very clearly, that if it is not true that Jesus Christ rose from the dead, then we the Christians are of all people the most unhappy. If none of that's true, and you seem to say it isn't, I have no quarrel with you. You're not going to come to my door trying to convince me either. Nor are you trying to get a tax break from the government. Nor are you trying to have it taught to my children in school. If all Christians were like you I wouldn't have to write the book.

SEWELL: Well, probably not, because I agree with almost everything that you say. But I still consider myself a Christian and a person of faith.

HITCHENS: Do you mind if I ask *you* a question? Faith in what? Faith in the resurrection?

SEWELL: The way I believe in the resurrection is I believe that one can go from a death in this life, in the sense of being dead to the world and dead to other people, and can be resurrected to new life. When I preach about Easter and the resurrection, it's in a metaphorical sense.

HITCHENS: I hate to say it—we've hardly been introduced—but maybe you are simply living on the inheritance of a monstrous fraud that was preached to millions of people as the literal truth—as you put it, "the ground of being."

SEWELL: Times change and, you know, people's beliefs change. I don't believe that you have to be fundamentalist and literalist to be a Christian. You do. You're something of a fundamentalist, actually.

HITCHENS: Well, I'm sorry, fundamentalist simply means those who think that the Bible is a serious book and should be taken seriously.

SEWELL: I take it very seriously. I have my grandmother's Bible and I still read it, but I don't take it as literal truth. I take it as metaphorical truth. The stories, the narrative, are what's important.

HITCHENS: But, then, show me what there is, ethically, in any religion that can't be duplicated by humanism. In other words, can you name me a single moral action performed or moral statement uttered by a person of faith that couldn't be just as well pronounced or undertaken by a civilian?

SEWELL: You're absolutely right. However, religion does inspire some people. You claim in the subtitle of your book that "religion poisons everything," but what about people like the Berrigan brothers, the Catholic priests who were jailed over and over again for their radical protesting of the Vietnam War? Or Bishop Romero, the nuns and priests who gave their lives supporting . . .

HITCHENS: They're all covered by the challenge I just presented to you. I know many people who . . .

SEWELL: Yeah, but these people claim to be motivated and sustained by their faith. Do you deny that?

HITCHENS: I don't claim. I don't deny it. I just don't respect. If someone says I'm doing this out of faith, I say, "Why don't you do it out of conviction?" I don't like the Berrigan brothers anyway. They're fanatical and they're pacifists who believe in the non-resistance to evil, which is itself an evil doctrine. And if Bishop Romero got as far as being an archbishop in El Salvador, he achieved the prestige carved out for him by an institution that has made El Salvador into an oppressive slave society.

SEWELL: That's true, but he did change.

HITCHENS: Well good for him. He needs to change a bit more. I know many, many, many people in El Salvador who have no religious faith of any kind who stuck up for human rights much longer, more consistently, and more bravely than he did. His prestige as an archbishop was meaningless to me.

SEWELL: Well, I can't argue with that.

HITCHENS: As it is for Martin Luther King. For example, he would've been much better off not invoking the nonsense story of Exodus, a story of massacre and the enslavement. He left us with a legacy where any clown or fraud or crook—Al Sharpton, Jesse Jackson, our new president's favorite priest in Chicago—who has the word reverend in front of his name can get an audience.

SEWELL: I would just say that this shows the fallen nature of people or, in secular language, the selfishness, egocentricity of all human beings. People are imperfect. But have you observed *any* redemptive aspects to religion?

HITCHENS: No, in the sense of the challenge I made: any good action by a religious person could be duplicated or matched, if not surpassed, by someone who didn't believe in God. And I would add the corollary question: Is there a wicked action performed by a religious person in the cause of their faith? And of course, you've already thought of several examples.

SEWELL: Yup, that's true.

HITCHENS: Religion makes kind people say unkind things: "I must prove my faith, so mutilate the genitals of my children." They wouldn't do that if God didn't tell them to do so. And it makes intelligent people say stupid things: "Condoms are worse than AIDS," for example. Things they wouldn't dream of saying if the pope didn't tell them to do that.

SEWELL: I agree and am appalled in the same way you are. Let me ask you this: The Greek myths, their fables, their folk tales that endured are not literally true, but there's great value in the universal truths that are taught just by the story itself. I see so much of scripture in a similar way, including, for example, the creation story. Can you agree with me that some of those stories are valuable just as metaphor?

HITCHENS: The creation story is ridiculous garbage and has given us a completely false picture of our origin as a species and the origins of the cosmos. If you want a good mythical story it would be the life of Socrates. We have no proof, as with Jesus, that he ever existed. We only know from witnesses to his life that he did. Like Jesus, he never wrote anything down. It doesn't matter to me whether he did or did not exist because we have his teachings, his method of thinking, and his extreme intellectual and moral courage. Anyone who can look me in the eye and say they prefer the story of Moses or Jesus or Mohammed to the life of Socrates is—I have to say it to you—intellectually defective. The great edition starts with Locutius and Epicurius, who work out that the world is made of atoms and is not created by any design. It goes through Socrates and through, well, Galileo,

Spinoza—people whose work is burned and despised by Jews and Christians and Muslims alike—through Voltaire to Darwin to, I'm abridging the story somewhat, but it's the last chapter of my book. It's a better tradition for people who think for themselves and who don't pray in aid of any supernatural authority. That's what you should be spending your life on, is in spreading and deepening that tradition.

SEWELL: You say that nonbelievers, "distrust anything that contradicts science or outrageous reason," that you respect free inquiry. I am a person of faith and absolutely agree with these two statements. But I do not believe that in order to be religious you have to disconnect your brain. Do you believe that and, if so, why?

HITCHENS: The smallest privilege of faith over reason is a betrayal. My daughter goes to a Quaker school, for example. Do I think that the Quakers are the same as Hezbollah? No, of course I don't, though I think there's a lot to be said against Quakerism morally, and what Quakers and Hezbollah do have in common is the idea that "faith" is an automatically good word. I think it's not. When people say, "I am a person of faith," they expect applause for it as we see in every election cycle. If I could make one change in the culture it would be to withhold that applause, to say, "Wait a minute, you just told me you're prepared to accept an enormous amount on no evidence whatsoever. Why are you thinking that that would impress me?" I have no use for it, when I could be spending time looking through a telescope or into a microscope and finding out the most extraordinary, wonderful things. People say faith can move mountains. Faith in what, by the way? You haven't said.

SEWELL: If you would like for me to talk a little bit about what I believe . . .

HITCHENS: Well I would, actually.

SEWELL: I don't know whether or not God exists in the first place, let me just say that. I certainly don't think that God is an old man in the sky, I don't believe that God intervenes to give me goodies if I ask for them.

HITCHENS: You don't believe he's an interventionist of any kind?

SEWELL: I'm kind of an agnostic on that one. God is a mystery to me. I choose to believe because—and this is a very practical thing for me—I seem to live with more integrity when I find myself accountable to something larger than myself. That thing larger than myself I call God, but it's a metaphor. That God is an emptiness out of which everything comes. Perhaps I would say "reality" or "what is" because we're trying to describe the infinite with language of the finite. My faith is that I put all that I am and all that I have on the line for that which I do not know.

HITCHENS: Fine. But I think that's a slight waste of what could honestly be in your case very valuable time. I don't want you to go away with the impression that I'm just a vulgar materialist. I do know that humans are also so made even though we are an evolved species whose closest cousins are chimpanzees. I know it's not enough for us to eat and so forth. We know how to think. We know how to laugh. We know we're going to die, which gives us a lot to think about, and we have a need for what I would call "the transcendent," or "the numinous," or even "the ecstatic" that comes out in love and music, poetry, and landscape. I wouldn't trust anyone who didn't respond to things of that sort. But I think the cultural task is to separate those impulses and those needs and desires from the supernatural and, above all, from the superstitious.

SEWELL: Could you talk about these two words that you just used, "transcendent" and "numinous"? Those two words are favorites of mine.

HITCHENS: Well, this would probably be very embarrassing, if you knew me. I can't compose or play music; I'm not that fortunate. But I can write and I can talk and sometimes when I'm doing either of these things I realize that I've written a sentence or uttered a thought that I didn't absolutely know I had in me . . . until I saw it on the page or heard myself say it. It was a sense that it wasn't all done by hand.

SEWELL: A gift?

HITCHENS: But, to me, that's the nearest I'm going to get to being an artist, which is the occupation I'd most like to have and the one, at last, I'm the most denied. But I think everybody has had the experience at some point when they feel that there's more to life than just matter. But I think it's very important to keep that under control and not to hand it over to be exploited by priests and shamans and rabbis and other riffraff.

SEWELL: You know, I think that that might be a religious impulse that you're talking about there.

HITCHENS: Well, it's absolutely not. It's a human one. It's part of the melancholy that we have in which we know that happiness is fleeting, and we know that life is brief, but we know that, nonetheless, life can be savored and that happiness, even of the ecstatic kind, is available to us. But we know that our life is essentially tragic as well. I'm absolutely not for handing over that very important department of our psyche to those who say, "Well, ah. Why didn't you say so before? God has a plan for you in mind." I have no time to waste on this planet being told what to do by those who think that God has given them instructions.

SEWELL: Those terms don't have to be attached to God. But I think a religious impulse is when you're just all of a sudden filled with the sense of thankfulness for something beautiful or for someone or perhaps—I use the word "numinous"—or when you're struck with some sense that there's something beyond you. It is a human phenomenon.

HITCHENS: I wrote a short book about the Parthenon and the sculpture of the Parthenon, the history of the building and so forth. Without that building, I would feel rather lost. If it were destroyed, for instance, I would feel that something really terrible had happened to the human species. But I'm able to appreciate the various symmetries and, um, magnificences of the Greek style without at all caring about the cults of Pallas Athena, the goddess in whose honor the building was erected or the Obsidian mysteries that were celebrated there or Athenian imperialism, in general—all those dead beliefs, as Christianity will one day be. It's a big cultural task for me to separate the cultural achievement that religion laid claim to from the claims of religion itself. No one's going to deny the role of religion in, for example, architecture or devotional painting (which, actually, I like that the least). In music, even though Verdi, it turns out, was not a believer, under that stimulus he could produce a pretty good requiem. The poetry of John Donne or George Herbert strikes me as having been produced by people who probably really believed what they were saying. I have to be impressed.

SEWELL: You write, "Literature, not scripture, sustains the mind and the soul." You use the word "soul" there as metaphor. What is a soul for you?

HITCHENS: It's what you might call "the x-factor"—I don't have a satisfactory term for it—it's what I mean by the element of us that isn't entirely materialistic: the numinous, the transcendent, the innocence of children (even though we know from Freud that childhood isn't as innocent as all that), the existence of love (which is, likewise, unquantifiable, but that anyone would be a fool who said it wasn't a powerful force), and so forth. I don't think the soul is immortal, or at least not immortal in individuals, but it may be immortal as an aspect of the human personality, because when I talk about what literature nourishes, it would be silly of me or reductionist to say that it nourishes the brain.

SEWELL: I wouldn't argue with you about the immortality of the soul. Were I back in a church again, I would love to have you in my church because you're so eloquent and I believe that some of your impulses—and, excuse me for saying so— are religious in the way I am religious. You may call it something else, but we agree in a lot of our thinking.

HITCHENS: I'm touched that you say, as some people have also said to me, that I've missed my vocation. But I actually don't think that I have. I would not be able to be this way if I was wearing robes or claiming authority that was other than human, that's a distinction that matters to me very much.

SEWELL: You have your role and it's a valuable one, so thank you for what you give to us.

HITCHENS: Well, thank you for asking. It's very good of you to be my hostess.

CHRISTOPHER HITCHENS: "YOU HAVE TO CHOOSE YOUR FUTURE REGRETS"

INTERVIEW BY ANDREW ANTHONY
THE GUARDIAN
NOVEMBER 13, 2010

I wasn't sure what, or perhaps whom, to expect as the door opened at Christopher Hitchens's top-floor apartment in downtown Washington. The last time I had interviewed the renowned polemicist, author, literary critic and new resident in the medical state he's called "Tumortown" was in 2005. On that occasion, after a 5 a.m. finish to our extravagantly lubricated conversation, it was I who had felt the pressing need of hospital attention.

Since then there have been two dramatic changes in his circumstances. The first was the international best-selling success of his 2007 anti-theist tome *God is Not Great*. After decades of acclaimed but essentially confined labour, Hitchens suddenly broke out to a mass audience, becoming arguably the global figurehead of the so-called New Atheists. Almost overnight he was upgraded from intellectual notoriety, as an outspoken supporter of the invasion of Iraq, to the business end of mainstream fame. In America, in particular, he has reached that rare position for a journalist of becoming a news story himself.

Unfortunately the news, which provided the second personal transformation, was that in June he was diagnosed with cancer of the esophagus, a malignancy whose survival ratings do not make soothing bedtime reading. As restraint is a quality for which neither Hitchens nor his critics are known, the ironies proved irresistible to many commentators. For the religiously zealous, the arch atheist suffering a mortal illness spoke of divine retribution—the unacknowledged irony being that belief in such a vindictive god served only to endorse Hitchens's thesis.

For more secular moralists, a different kind of cosmic accountancy was at work. The celebrated drinker and smoker who once claimed that "booze and fags are happiness" had succumbed to a cancer most often associated with drinking and smoking. Having previously gone so far as to promote the benefits of teenage smoking, he offered a public recantation of sorts. "I might as well say to anyone watching," he announced in a TV interview, "if you can hold it down on the smokes and the cocktails you may be well advised to do so."

Hitchens had already impregnated the story with pre-emptive meaning in his prologue to his recent memoir, *Hitch-22*, in which he meditated on the unpredictable incursion of death. One motivation to undertake the book, he confessed, was the need to do so before it was "too 'late.'" As he wrote those words, he had no knowledge of the tumour growing in his esophagus, which has metastasised in his lymph nodes and lung. It was not until he was on a promotional tour for the book that he fell ill and was diagnosed.

There followed the minor spectacle of prayer groups invoking the unbeliever in their spiritual communications and even, in September, the informal designation of an "Everybody pray for Hitchens day." While avoiding any direct involvement, the writer professed himself touched by the attention. But for such an astute connoisseur of the form, these ironies were no doubt just a little too resounding for Hitchens to appreciate.

On top of which there was the distant thud of literary biography. One of Hitchens's great heroes is George Orwell, who no sooner produced his signature achievements (*Animal Farm*, Nineteen Eighty-Four) than was confronted with the prospect of his premature demise. Orwell cut a frail, bedridden figure towards the end of his short life, a fate that seemed to confirm his ascetic form of courage.

All very well for the man who nursed his TB alone in the damp reclusion of Jura, but infirmity was never going to be an image that sat well with Hitchens, a walking definition of the cosmopolitan *bon viveur*. The early post-chemo photographs and appearances were not encouraging. Without his trademark foppish fringe, he seemed to have undergone a Samsonian reduction. The few wisps of hair remaining mocked the mischievously boyish countenance that had duly withdrawn behind gloomy eyes. He looked old and battered. He looked like a 61-year-old man with stage-four cancer.

He'd told me by email that he had good and bad days. As I'd pushed him for the interview, it was with a certain trepidation that I stood clutching an effete bottle of white wine—I assumed that his usual tipple of whisky had been removed from the menu. At first, when he greeted me, I wasn't entirely convinced it was one of his better days. Although he looked fitter and sharper than he had in those earlier images, having lost a little weight and with his head now more flatteringly bald, the apartment was in darkness and he invited me in to watch the sunset. It all seemed rather forlorn.

If it triggered his cancer, burning the candle at both

ends, as he recently remarked, also produced a "lovely light." The golden twilight over the American capital possessed its own illuminating charm, not least in the way that it seemed to recharge Hitchens. So it was that for a considerable part of the next 24 hours he held forth with unhesitating eloquence on a wealth of subjects, including the Iraq war and its likely aftermath, the global jihadist threat, his love of debate, romance, his illness and, of course, the persistently intrusive claims of religion.

When he initially became ill, Hitchens thought that he was suffering from exhaustion, brought on by overwork and age. "I knew something was wrong," he says. "I kept saying to myself, when the book tour is over I really will go and see a doctor."

He collapsed first on the New York leg of his tour, and had fluid drained from around his heart. Then an oncologist performed a biopsy. Most authors would have called off the rest of the dates at this juncture. But Hitchens went on to Florida, Chicago and Philadelphia, before collapsing again, this time at Boston airport, a venue he recommends for a speedy medical response.

The surgeons took a lump of tumour for analysis and opened what's known as a "window" in the pericardium to allow fluid drainage. Since then he's been undergoing chemotherapy at three-week intervals. The tumour has shrunk, but not sufficiently for radiotherapy, and he was about to start a new course of a different cocktail of drugs. At the same time he's been having his genome sequenced and that of the tumour—though, since this sci-fi approach to cancer treatment is still in its infancy, it is unlikely to offer any help to Hitchens.

"The worst days," he says, "are when you feel foggy in the head—chemo-brain they call it. It's awful because you feel boring. As well as bored. And stupid. And resigned. You don't have any motive, which is bad. You don't care what's going to happen to you. That lasts sometimes two days. And when that comes with nausea—even if you have eaten, you have to go and be sick—it's very upsetting."

But there are also some more favourable signs. For instance, he hasn't yet had any trouble swallowing, a problem frequently associated with esophageal cancer. And his immune system remains strong: "I haven't picked up a sneeze or anything like that."

Which is just as well, because Hitchens was never going to be a natural candidate for a prune-juice and brown-rice lifestyle. He was grateful for my white wine, but only because that's what I drink and he was low on stocks. For himself he poured a generous measure of Johnnie Walker. None of his doctors, he says, has issued any kind of fatwa on booze, though you sense he probably hasn't demanded a ruling.

Whatever his health regime, it doesn't appear to have affected his work levels. The pugnacious weekly *Slate* column, the far-reaching literary essays for the *Atlantic Monthly*, and the *Vanity Fair* dispatches are all filed on time. And he continues to participate in public debates. Last month in New York he sliced through the Islamic scholar Tariq Ramadan's problematising evasions with stinging precision, and later this month he's taking on Tony Blair in Toronto.

He disputes his industriousness on the grounds that he's not currently writing a book. "I spend a lot of time asleep or lying down." Yet the spacious apartment he shares with his wife, the writer Carol Blue, and their 18-year-old daughter, Antonia, shows few signs of recuperative comforts. With its bare floorboards, sparse furniture, baby grand piano and teetering stalagmites of books, it resembles something a Hollywood set designer might have come up with had she been asked to create an intellectual's lair.

He's said before that his life is his writing, which includes priority over his family, but perhaps it would be more accurate to say that his life is an argument in which writing takes the lead role. It's notable that there's scarcely any mention of his wife or his children or former lovers in his memoir. He stated in the book that this was out of respect for others' privacy. If he had named one woman, he adds, he would have had to go into detail about them all. "Couldn't do it selectively, it would lead to nothing but pain."

One of the women he didn't name was Anna Wintour, the legendarily glacial editor of American *Vogue*. They had a year-long affair in the mid-70s.

"It was transatlantic, very stormy, tempestuous, passionate," he says, "all of this enhanced by having to fly the Atlantic the whole time. Otherwise it might not have gone on for so long because really, although she's amazing, we didn't have much in common."

Other than fashion, I joke. Among his many struggles, the one waged against the tyranny of the pressed and laundered outfit should not be overlooked. Still, the absence of women in the foreground of his memoir leaves the impression of a life consciously determined by the intellect, rather than haphazardly shaped by emotions. It's an effect that's underlined in his writing by a Zelig-like presence at the great moments of history, as though they are the dots that join together to form an inexorable continuity.

He shakes his head. "Even with all the advantages of retrospect, and a lot of witnesses dead and gone, you can't make your life look as if you intended it or you were consistent. All you can show is how you dealt with various hands."

In America it's been suggested by some religious types that his condition could prompt a revision of his atheism. It's not a hypothesis to which he grants much respect.

"So now I know that there's another life in my body that can't outlive me but can kill me, it's the perfect moment to gratefully acknowledge that I'm a product of a cosmic design? Who thinks up these arguments? Actually it's an insulting question: 'I hear you're dying. Well wouldn't it be a good time to get rid of your beliefs?' Try it on them and see how they would like it. 'Christian, right? Cancer of the tits?' 'Well, yes, since you ask.' 'Well, can I suggest you now drop all that tripe?'"

In Britain, I say, the notion that he will undergo some kind of deathbed conversion has minimal traction. What you find more often here is the accusation that the New Atheism, as expounded by Hitchens and his fellow bestsellers, Richard Dawkins, Sam Harris and Daniel Dennett, is a "militant" or even "fundamentalist" attack on the numinous and the unknowable.

Hitchens once wrote a line that has almost gained the status of philosophical epigram or even scientific dictum:

"What can be asserted without evidence can be dismissed without evidence." Although it echoes Wittgenstein's famous injunction regarding the ineffable—"Whereof we cannot speak, thereof we must be silent"—Hitchens's version is less a "no entry" sign than a civic reminder to place rubbish in the bin.

In fact, you could say that in *God is Not Great* Hitchens ignored his own advice by conducting lengthy theological and historical research to assemble his case. His beef, in any event, is not really against faith itself, but against the way that all faiths are compelled to make irrational demands on believers and non-believers alike.

Hitchens dislikes the "New Atheist" title. "It isn't really new," he says, "except it coincides with huge advances made in the natural sciences. And there's been an unusually violent challenge to pluralist values by the supporters of at least one monotheism apologised for quite often by the sympathisers of others. Then they say we're fundamentalists. A stupid idea like that is hard to kill because any moron can learn it in 10 seconds and repeat it as if for the first time. But since there isn't a single position that any of us holds on anything that depends upon an assertion that can't be challenged, I guess that will die out or they'll get bored of it."

As for the notion that his brand of atheism is reductive or joyless, it's religion, he contests, that is "cosmically hopeless, as is all the related masochism that goes with it—you've got to spend your entire life making up for the vermin you are. What is that if not degrading? We don't do that to people. We say you may as well know you're a primate, but take heart, primates are capable of great things."

Nonetheless, Hitchens mentions a "narrow but quite deep difference" between himself and Dawkins. Unlike the evangelical biologist, he has no wish to convert everyone in the world to his point of view, even if it were possible. In other words, he savours the counterargument. Like John Stuart Mill, he is aware of the empty end of achieved objectives. The true satisfaction lies in the means. Although Hitchens is often seen as a provocateur or a contrarian, and both are indeed aspects of his character, at heart he's incurably in love with the dialectic.

He cut his teeth on dialectical materialism as a teenage Trotskyist, and it was the analytical method that eventually put paid to any allegiance, as it were, to the political madness. The past 40 years have amounted to a long and serpentine political journey. As he relates in his memoir, it started out at Oxford with his keeping "two sets of books," one for the puritanical group of revolutionary socialists with whom he campaigned against the Vietnam War, and the other for the conservative socialites with whom he caroused at black-tie balls. And it reached its furthest distance from origin with his support for George W. Bush and the second Iraq war.

Along the way, he says, "I learned that very often the most intolerant and narrow-minded people are the ones who congratulate themselves on their tolerance and open-mindedness. Amazing. My conservative friends look at me and say, 'Welcome to the club. What took you so long?' Well that's what it took and I think it's worth recording."

The hinge events, of course, were the 9/11 attacks on New York and Washington. He had previously held positions that were unpopular on the left—preferring the British government to the Argentinian fascist junta during the Falklands conflict, and calling for American intervention to stop the ethnic cleansing in Bosnia—but his support for the toppling of the Taliban in Afghanistan proved to be a step too far for his anti-imperialist comrades.

Hitchens genuinely believes radical or jihadist Islam to be an existential threat to civilisation. First because it is a pronounced enemy of free speech and social liberty and has succeeded in intimidating and silencing civilians across "an extraordinary number of countries in Europe" and the rest of the world. And second, he says, "because it has potential access to weapons of mass destruction." In the end, he argues, there are no pain-free options. You have to choose which future regret you're going to have.

"I was at a Hezbollah rally in Beirut about two and a half years ago," he says. "Very striking. Everyone should go. But of the many things that impressed me about it, having the mushroom cloud as the party flag in an election campaign was the main one. You wouldn't want to look back and think, I wish I'd noticed that being run up. Now I can give you all the reasons that it's bombast on their part. Still, I know which regret I'd rather have."

There appear to be two main criticisms of this stance. Either people think he's a bonkers Islamophobe—though many who do were content enough to leave Muslims to their bloody fate in Bosnia—or they believe such antagonistic talk only serves to create the problem it seeks to prevent. Hitchens is contemptuous of the former, but scathing of the latter. He says that those who tell him to tread more softly believe that the price of not doing so is more violence. "Oh I see, so you're always aware when you're contesting the holders of this view of the threat that lies behind it? Would you care for their opinions if it wasn't for that? Or are you telling me you'd be reading their stuff just for the sheer pleasure of it. I don't think so. If you say that this looks like war, you're accused of liking it. Not true. Demonstrably not true."

Demonstrably? Certainly he can sound like he enjoys the conflict. He has said that he experienced "a feeling of exhilaration" while watching the World Trade Center collapse on 11 September. "Here we are then," he later recalled thinking, "in a war to the finish between everything I love and everything I hate. Fine. We will win and they will lose."

He says the exhilaration was born of a sudden if overdue sense of clarity.

"What I felt is that we'd been suffering from all this for some time. And yet people's main interest seemed to be in ignoring it or denying it, or if they were politicians or soldiers, running away from it: abandoning Somalia, leaving Afghanistan to rot, trying to subsume Islamism into multiculturalism. I thought: until yesterday, they knew they were at war, and we didn't. And now we do: of course that's exhilarating. It was the feeling that the somnambulance was over. Of course it turned out to be a very brief wake-up call, followed by a very long nap: 'Turned over in bed briefly. It's 8:59? No, it can't possibly be!'"

If 9/11 was the decree nisi, then the divorce from the left was made absolute by the war in Iraq. He had been a persuasive opponent of the first Gulf war in 1991, arguing that

Bush senior was not liberating Kuwait but simply restoring the status quo. Slowly he changed his mind, and he describes the process:

"I said that Bush [senior] may have used the rhetoric of anti-fascism but he didn't mean it. And then I said, yeah, but what if he had meant it? Would I therefore be obliged by my own argument to be in favour? The answer was 'yes.' And then I said, well what do you care how they argue? You should be arguing it yourself. And I found I couldn't get out of that."

It's an instructive piece of reasoning. For while it suggests he remained true to his dialectical word by examining the counterargument, it's also a kind of a first-principles assessment of principles. As such it could be applied to countless other situations. For example, should the west have intervened in Cambodia when stories first began to emerge of the genocide taking place there under the Khmer Rouge? "I don't think there was a policy," he says, a little lamely, "so I can't say that there should have been one. I don't think it's a real question."

His only major regret, as far as remaining silent goes, is what he didn't say about Robert Mugabe. "That makes me wince. More than wince. I'd met him a couple of times and I knew that he had in him a terrible capacity for fanaticism, absolutism, and I didn't say as much about that as I could have done. If I asked myself about why I didn't, I'm sure the answer is because I didn't want to give ammunition to the other side."

As an aside on Mugabe, he makes one of those observations that are so precisely to the point that you wonder why so few other commentators ever get round to coming to it. "Darfur, Zimbabwe, Burma, North Korea, anywhere that the concept of human rights doesn't exist, it's always the Chinese at backstop. And always for reasons that you could write down in three words: blood for oil."

But the problem with Hitchens's inductive reasoning about Iraq is that it didn't and couldn't take into account future outcomes—namely the relative likelihood of death and destruction. In the light of what unfolded in the wake of the occupation, these were the matters that I wanted to put to him the following day.

First, though, there was dinner. We walked to a local restaurant where Hitchens knows the barman and the barman knows what Hitchens drinks, and I asked whether his cancer diagnosis had altered his political outlook at all. He looked mystified at the question, but I explained that he used to say that he woke up angry, full of disgust at the world. Was it still possible to feel so strongly about external enemies when the internal one had taken such malevolent root in his body?

"It's the sort of alternative that doesn't present itself to you," he says. "You don't think, 'Why do I care when I could be thinking about my daunting nemesis?'"

The banality of cancer seems to irk him almost as much as its lethality. Lacking any dialectical substance, it affords few opportunities to escape platitude or avoid cliché. It's a big subject, but it's essentially small talk, and Hitchens's style requires the elevated registers of the epic and the ironic. Anything less is like asking a high-wire artist to perform his act at ground level.

Yet his engagement remains unusually engaging, in large part because with him it's never just about politics. His frame of cultural interests is far too large to be squeezed into the straitjacket of dogma and doctrine. He chided me a couple of times for not asking him about his first love, literature. "I wish people would put in a bit more of that because it's also what I think of when I say grand things like defending civilisation."

It's no coincidence that the political thinkers he most often references are also gifted writers: Orwell, Arthur Koestler, Thomas Paine, even Thomas Jefferson. The first two, like Hitchens, committed anti-totalitarians, and the second pair voices from the only revolution—the American—whose praises he continues to sing.

Hitchens's friend Ian Buruma wrote a damning review of *Hitch-22*, in which he noted that Hitchens displays "a tendency toward adulation and loathing [that] comes naturally with the weakness for great causes."

Was that fair?

"I think that probably is true of me, that I can be 110 percent for or against people," he says, pausing meaningfully. "I don't know whether that's meant as a criticism or not."

We repair back to the apartment for a nightcap or two, and I fear it is I, the ostensibly well one, who crashes first. The spare room had only recently been vacated by Patrick Cockburn, the distinguished foreign correspondent, old friend of Hitchens and savage critic of the Iraqi occupation. Clearly the breach with the "other side" is not quite so decisive up close and personal as it might sometimes appear from afar.

The following morning Hitchens rises late, as is his routine nowadays, and after working for an hour or two, reconvenes our discussion over lunch. We sit in the dining room with the window open on a distinctly chilly autumn afternoon. He's wearing just a thin shirt, while I shiver in a thick pullover. Not for the first time, I feel a twinge of pity for that tumour. Does it *realise* what it's up against?

A few days before we met, Tariq Aziz, Saddam's former deputy, was sentenced to death in Iraq for suppressing Shia religious parties during the Ba'ath rule. This surely wasn't the bright future for Iraq that the trenchant secularist and opponent of capital punishment had in mind back in 2003. He agrees that it's depressing news. Nor is he confident that things won't deteriorate after the coalition has departed.

"The best one can do is say that we've given the Iraqis the chance to produce a constitution, independent courts and a free press. They can keep it if they want but the parties of God may veto that. Unless we're directly requested by a functioning government backed by a functioning parliamentary vote to stay on, we have to leave it to them now."

So if the parties of God gain control, Iran's influence increases and human rights further decline, will it still all have been worth the loss of life and limb?

"Oh yes, I definitely think so," he replies without vacillation, "and not just for the humanitarian reasons. There are all kinds of reasons that don't get discussed and are harder to quantify."

He points out something he says opponents of the war always fail to mention: the success of an autonomous Kurdistan. But he also says that the discovery of oil around Baghdad has transformed the material basis for political control. "There's a petro-chemical reason for federalism now. If the oil laws were enforced properly by province, it could be as rich as Kuwait. The Saudis and the Iranians don't want a revived Iraqi oil industry because it will undercut them. You could have a modern Middle Eastern country or a parties-of-God failed state."

The point, I say, is that you can't make countries take the right path.

"No, again, since one is always going to regret something, you have to decide in advance what it will be. OK, I'm glad we're not having an inquest now, as we would be, into why we allowed a Rwanda or a Congo to develop on the Gulf, an imploding Iraq right in front of our eyes, a vortex of violence and meltdown, a whole society beggared and fractured and traumatised, waiting to fall to pieces."

The problem with this picture, of course, is that many people believe that it exactly describes what has taken place since the invasion. Hitchens maintains that the situation is better than it would otherwise have been, and to the extent that it's worse, the responsibility lies with al-Qaida.

"Trying to destroy the Christian community, strategy of tension, trying to start a civil war," he says, listing al-Qaida's nihilistic programme, "and people act as if those casualties should be on my conscience. I won't have that. For one thing, it absolves those who have done it of their guilt."

I try to argue that it overstates the case to suggest, as some of his more deranged critics claim, that he is somehow personally responsible for the tens of thousands of lost lives in Iraq. After all, had he not existed, would history have taken a different path?

To his credit, he refuses to accept that get-out. As he does in his memoir, he restates his role, along with people such as Peter Galbraith and Kenan Makiya (he insists Ahmed Chalabi's part has been "ridiculously exaggerated") in helping to persuade Washington of the need for regime change. But he also says that, even if he had negligible or no effect, "you should act as if your opinion might have made the difference. You don't have to be a megalomaniac to do that. And to say that you feel to that extent responsible, without making a parade of your feelings."

What's beyond doubt is that Hitchens's sense of optimism and purpose in 2002 in Washington was never going to be matched by the post-invasion plan in Iraq in 2003. He has no quarrel with the fact that the occupation was badly handled. "As Peter [Galbraith] said, you never get a second chance to make a good first impression. Tragic. But I mean tragic."

He leaves the room briefly to deal with a domestic issue and I take the opportunity to close the window. When he returns, he opens it with a knowing smile.

"I'll bring you an overcoat," he quips.

We continue talking for another couple of hours on everything from the Russian revolution to the Bay of Pigs, from the Spanish civil war to Tony Blair. In the end, it's only my need to catch a plane that brings the discussion to a close. With Hitchens, though, the argument will continue, first with himself and then, if need be, with the world. His intemperate style is not to everyone's tastes, but as he has often remarked, you can't produce light without heat. To those of us who admire his clarity of thought, if not always his conclusions, it is indeed a lovely light. And I'm pleased to say that on a cold November day in Tumortown, it showed little sign of fading.

THE LAST INTERVIEW:
"NEVER BE AFRAID OF STRIDENCY"

INTERVIEW BY RICHARD DAWKINS
NEW STATESMAN
DECEMBER 2011

DAWKINS: Do you have any memories of life at *New Statesman*?

HITCHENS: Not that I want to impart. It seems like a different world and a different magazine and it happened to a different person. I'd love them to interview me one day about it, for an edition about the role of the *Statesman*, but I'd really rather you and I focus on the pulse of the issue, which is obviously our common cause.

DAWKINS: I've been reading some of your recent collections of essays—I'm astounded by your sheer erudition. You seem to have read absolutely everything. I can't think of anybody since Aldous Huxley who's so well read.

HITCHENS: It may strike some people as being broad but it's possibly at the cost of being a bit shallow. I became a journalist because one didn't have to specialise. I remember once going to an evening with Umberto Eco talking to Susan Sontag and the definition of the word "polymath" came up. Eco said it was his ambition to be a polymath; Sontag challenged him and said the definition of a polymath is someone who's interested in everything and nothing else. I was encouraged in my training to read widely—to flit and sip, as Bertie [Wooster] puts it—and I think I've got good memory retention. I retain what's interesting to me, but I don't have a lot of strategic depth. A lot of reviewers have said, to the point of embarrassing me, that I'm in the class of Edmund Wilson or even George Orwell. It really does remind me that I'm not. But it's something to at least have had the comparison made—it's better than I expected when I started.

DAWKINS: As an Orwell scholar, you must have a particular view of North Korea, Stalin, the Soviet Union, and you must get irritated—perhaps even more than I do—by the constant refrain we hear: "Stalin was an atheist."

HITCHENS: We don't know for sure that he was. Hitler definitely wasn't. There is a possibility that Himmler was. It's very unlikely but it wouldn't make any difference, either way. There's no mandate in atheism for any particular kind of politics, anyway.

DAWKINS: The people who did Hitler's dirty work were almost all religious.

HITCHENS: I'm afraid the SS's relationship with the Catholic Church is something the Church still has to deal with and does not deny.

DAWKINS: Can you talk a bit about that—the relationship of Nazism with the Catholic Church?

HITCHENS: The way I put it is this: if you're writing about the history of the 1930s and the rise of totalitarianism, you can take out the word "fascist," if you want, for Italy, Portugal, Spain, Czechoslovakia and Austria and replace it with "extreme right Catholic party." Almost all of those regimes were in place with the help of the Vatican and with understandings from the Holy See. It's not denied. These understandings quite often persisted after the Second World War was over and extended to comparable regimes in Argentina and elsewhere.

DAWKINS: But there were individual priests who did good things.

HITCHENS: Not very many. You would know their names if there were more of them. When it comes to National Socialism, there's no question there's a mutation, a big one—the Nazis wanted their own form of worship. Just as they thought they were a separate race, they wanted their own religion. They dug out the Norse gods, all kinds of extraordinary myths and legends from the old sagas. They wanted to control the churches. They were willing to make a deal with them. The first deal Hitler made with the Catholic Church was the Konkordat. The Church agreed to dissolve its political party and he got control over German education, which was a pretty good deal. Celebrations of his birthday were actually by order from the pulpit. When Hitler survived an assassination attempt, prayers were said, and so forth. But there's no doubt about it, [the Nazis] wanted control—and they were willing to clash with the churches to get it. There's another example. You swore on Almighty God that you would never break your oath to the Führer. This is not even secular, let alone atheist.

DAWKINS: There was also grace before meals, personally thanking Adolf Hitler.

HITCHENS: I believe there was. Certainly, you can hear the oath being taken—there are recordings of it—but this, Richard, is a red herring. It's not even secular. They're changing the subject.

DAWKINS: But it comes up over and over again.

HITCHENS: You mentioned North Korea. It is, in every sense, a theocratic state. It's almost supernatural, in that the births of the [ruling] Kim family are considered to be mysterious and accompanied by happenings. It's a necrocracy or mausolocracy, but there's no possible way you could say it's a secular state, let alone an atheist one. Attempts to found new religions should attract our scorn just as much as the alliances with the old ones do. All they're saying is that you can't claim Hitler was distinctively or specifically Christian: "Maybe if he had gone on much longer, he would have de-Christianised a bit more." This is all a complete fog of nonsense. It's bad history and it's bad propaganda.

DAWKINS: And bad logic, because there's no connection between atheism and doing horrible things, whereas there easily can be a connection in the case of religion, as we see with modern Islam.

HITCHENS: To the extent that they are new religions—Stalin worship and Kim Il-sungism—we, like all atheists, regard them with horror.

DAWKINS: You debated with Tony Blair. I'm not sure I watched that. I love listening to you [but] I can't bear listening to . . . Well, I mustn't say that. I think he did come over as rather nice on that evening.

HITCHENS: He was charming, that evening. And during the day, as well.

DAWKINS: What was your impression of him?

HITCHENS: You can only have one aim per debate. I had two in debating with Tony Blair. The first one was to get him to admit that it was not done—the stuff we complain of—in only the name of religion. That's a cop-out. The authority is in the text. Second, I wanted to get him to admit, if possible, that giving money to a charity or organising a charity does not vindicate a cause. I got him to the first one and I admired his honesty. He was asked by the interlocutor at about half-time: "Which of Christopher's points strikes you as the best?" He said: "I have to admit, he's made his case, he's right. This stuff, there is authority for it in the canonical texts, in Islam, Judaism." At that point, I'm ready to fold—I've done what I want for the evening. We did debate whether Catholic charities and so on were a good thing and I said: "They are but they don't prove any point and some of them are only making up for damage done." For example, the Church had better spend a lot of money doing repair work on its AIDS policy in Africa, [to make up for preaching] that condoms don't prevent disease or, in some cases, that they spread it. It is iniquitous. It has led to a lot of people dying, horribly. Also, I've never looked at some of the ground operations of these charities—apart from Mother Teresa—but they do involve a lot of proselytising, a lot of propaganda. They're not just giving out free stuff. They're doing work to recruit.

DAWKINS: And Mother Teresa was one of the worst offenders?

HITCHENS: She preached that poverty was a gift from God. And she believed that women should not be given control over the reproductive cycle. Mother Teresa spent her whole life making sure that the one cure for poverty we know is sound was not implemented. So Tony Blair knows this but he doesn't have an answer. If I say, "Your Church preaches against the one cure for poverty," he doesn't deny it, but he doesn't affirm it either. But remember, I did start with a text and I asked him to comment on it first, but he never did. Cardinal Newman said he would rather the whole world and everyone in it be painfully destroyed and condemned for ever to eternal torture than one sinner go unrebuked for the stealing of a sixpence. It's right there in the centre of the *Apologia*. The man whose canonisation Tony had been campaigning for. You put these discrepancies in front of him and he's like all the others. He keeps two sets of books. And this is also, even in an honest person, shady.

DAWKINS: It's like two minds, really. One notices this with some scientists.

HITCHENS: I think we all do it a bit.

DAWKINS: Do we?

HITCHENS: We're all great self-persuaders.

DAWKINS: But do we hold such extreme contradictions in our heads?

HITCHENS: We like to think our colleagues would point them out, in our group, anyway. No one's pointed out to me in reviewing my God book *God Is Not Great* that there's a flat discrepancy between the affirmation he makes on page X and the affirmation he makes on page Y.

DAWKINS: But they do accuse you of being a contrarian, which you've called yourself . . .

HITCHENS: Well, no, I haven't. I've disowned it. I was asked to address the idea of it and I began by saying it's got grave shortcomings as an idea, but I am a bit saddled with it.

DAWKINS: I've always been very suspicious of the left-right dimension in politics.

HITCHENS: Yes; it's broken down with me.

DAWKINS: It's astonishing how much traction the left-right continuum [has] . . . If you know what someone thinks about the death penalty or abortion, then you generally know what they think about everything else. But you clearly break that rule.

HITCHENS: I have one consistency, which is [being] against the totalitarian—on the left and on the right. The totalitarian, to me, is the enemy—the one that's absolute, the one that wants control over the inside of your head, not just your actions and your taxes. And the origins of that are theocratic, obviously. The beginning of that is the idea that there is a supreme leader, or infallible pope, or a chief rabbi, or whatever, who can ventriloquise the divine and tell us what to do. That has secular forms with gurus and dictators, of course, but it's essentially the same. There have been some thinkers—Orwell is pre-eminent—who understood that, unfortunately, there is innate in humans a strong tendency to worship, to become abject. So we're not just fighting the dictators. We're criticising our fellow humans for trying to short-cut, to make their lives simpler, by surrendering and saying, "[If] you offer me bliss, of course I'm going to give up some of my mental freedom for that." We say it's a false bargain: you'll get nothing. You're a fool.

DAWKINS: That part of you that was, or is, of the radical left is always against the totalitarian dictators.

HITCHENS: Yes. I was a member of the Trotskyist group—for us, the socialist movement could only be revived if it was purged of Stalinism . . . It's very much a point for our view that Stalinism was a theocracy.

DAWKINS: One of my main beefs with religion is the way they label children as a "Catholic child" or a "Muslim child." I've become a bit of a bore about it.

HITCHENS: You must never be afraid of that charge, any more than stridency.

DAWKINS: I will remember that.

HITCHENS: If I was strident, it doesn't matter—I was a jobbing hack, I bang my drum. You have a discipline in which you are very distinguished. You've educated a lot of people; nobody denies that, not even your worst enemies. You see your discipline being attacked and defamed and attempts made to drive it out.

Stridency is the least you should muster . . . It's the shame of your colleagues that they don't form ranks and say, "Listen, we're going to defend our colleagues from these appalling and obfuscating elements." If you go on about something, the worst thing the English will say about you, as we both know—as we can say of them, by the way—is that they're boring.

DAWKINS: Indeed. Only this morning, I was sent a copy of [advice from] a British government website, called something like "The Responsibilities of Parents." One of these responsibilities was "determine the child's religion." Literally, determine. It means establish, cause . . . I couldn't ask for a clearer illustration, because, sometimes, when I make my complaint about this, I'm told nobody actually does label children Catholic children or Muslim children.

HITCHENS: Well, the government does. It's borrowed, as far as I can see, in part from British imperial policy, in turn borrowed from Ottoman and previous empires—you classify your new subjects according to their faith. You can be an Ottoman citizen but you're a Jewish one or an Armenian Christian one. And some of these faiths tell their children that the children of other faiths are going to hell. I think we can't ban that, nor can we call it "hate speech," which I'm dubious about anyway, but there should be a wrinkle of disapproval.

DAWKINS: I would call it mental child abuse.

HITCHENS: I can't find a way, as a libertarian, of saying that people can't raise their children, as they say, according to their rights. But the child has rights and society does, too. We don't allow female—and I don't think we should countenance male—genital mutilation.

Now, it would be very hard to say that you can't tell your child that they are lucky and they have joined the one true faith. I don't see how you stop it. I only think the rest of society should look at it with a bit of disapproval, which it doesn't. If you're a Mormon and you run for office and say, "Do you believe in the golden plates that were dug up by Joseph Smith?"—which [Mitt] Romney hasn't been asked yet—sorry, you're going to get mocked. You're going to get laughed at.

DAWKINS: There is a tendency among liberals to feel that religion should be off the table.

HITCHENS: Or even that there's anti-religious racism, which I think is a terrible limitation.

DAWKINS: Romney has questions to answer.

HITCHENS: Certainly, he does. The question of Mormon racism did come up, to be fair, and the Church did very belatedly make amends for saying what, in effect, it had been saying: that black people's souls weren't human, quite. They timed it suspiciously for the passage of legislation. Well, OK, then they grant the right of society to amend [the legislation]. To that extent, they're opportunists.

DAWKINS: But what about the daftness of Mormonism? The fact that Joseph Smith was clearly a charlatan—

HITCHENS: I know, it's extraordinary.

DAWKINS: I think there is a convention in America that you don't tackle somebody about their religion.

HITCHENS: Yes, and in a way it's attributed to pluralism. And so, to that extent, one wants to respect it, but I think it can be exploited. By many people, including splinter-group Mormons who still do things like plural marriage and, very repulsively, compulsory dowries—they basically give away their daughters, often to blood relatives. And also kinship marriages that are too close. This actually won't quite do. When it is important, they tend to take refuge in: "You're attacking my fundamental right." I don't think they really should be allowed that.

DAWKINS: Do you think America is in danger of becoming a theocracy?

HITCHENS: No, I don't. The people who we mean when we talk about that—maybe the extreme Protestant evangelicals, who do want a God-run America and believe it was founded on essentially fundamentalist Protestant principles—I think they may be the most overrated threat in the country.

DAWKINS: Oh, good.

HITCHENS: They've been defeated everywhere. Why is this? In the 1920s, they had a string of victories. They banned the sale, manufacture and distribution and consumption of alcohol. They made it the constitution. They more or less managed to ban immigration from countries that had non-Protestant, non-white majorities. From these victories, they have never recovered. They'll never recover from [the failure of] Prohibition. It was their biggest defeat. They'll never recover from the Scopes trial. Every time they've tried [to introduce the teaching of creationism], the local school board or the parents or the courts have thrown it out and it's usually because of the work of people like you, who have shown that it's nonsense. They try to make a free speech question out of it but they will fail with that, also. People don't want to come from the town or the state or the county that gets laughed at.

DAWKINS: Yes.

HITCHENS: In all my tours around the South, it's amazing how many people—Christians as well—want to disprove the idea that they're all in thrall to people like [the fundamentalist preacher Jerry] Falwell. They don't want to be a laughing stock.

DAWKINS: Yes.

HITCHENS: And if they passed an ordinance saying there will be prayer in school every morning from now on, one of two things would happen: it would be overthrown in no time by all the courts, with barrels of laughter heaped over it, or people would say: "Very well, we're starting with Hindu prayer on Monday." They would regret it so bitterly that there are days when I wish they would have their own way for a short time.

DAWKINS: Oh, that's very cheering.

HITCHENS: I'm a bit more worried about the extreme, reactionary nature of the papacy now. But that again doesn't seem to command very big allegiance among the American congregation. They are disobedient on contraception, flagrantly; on divorce; on gay marriage, to an extraordinary degree that I wouldn't have predicted; and they're only holding firm on abortion, which, in my opinion, is actually a very strong moral question and shouldn't be decided lightly. I feel very squeamish about it. I believe that the unborn child is a real concept, in other words. We needn't go there, but I'm not a complete abortion-on-demand fanatic. I think it requires a bit of reflection. But anyway, even on that, the Catholic Communion is very agonised. And also, [when] you go and debate with them, very few of them could tell you very much about what the catechism really is. It's increasingly cultural Catholicism.

DAWKINS: That is true, of course.

HITCHENS: So, really, the only threat from religious force in America is the same as it is, I'm afraid, in many other countries—from outside. And it's jihadism, some of it home-grown, but some of that is so weak and so self-discrediting.

DAWKINS: It's more of a problem in Britain.

HITCHENS: And many other European countries, where its alleged root causes are being allowed slightly too friendly an interrogation, I think. Make that much too friendly.

DAWKINS: Some of our friends are so worried about Islam that they're prepared to lend support to Christianity as a kind of bulwark against it.

HITCHENS: I know many Muslims who, in leaving the faith, have opted to go . . . to Christianity or via it to non-belief. Some of them say it's the personality of Jesus of Nazareth. The mild and meek one, as compared to the rather farouche, physical, martial, rather greedy . . .

DAWKINS: Warlord.

HITCHENS: . . . Muhammad. I can see that that might have an effect.

DAWKINS: Do you ever worry that if we win and, so to speak, destroy Christianity, that vacuum would be filled by Islam?

HITCHENS: No, in a funny way, I don't worry that we'll win. All that we can do is make absolutely sure that people know there's a much more wonderful and interesting and beautiful alternative. No, I don't think that Europe would fill up with Muslims as it emptied of Christians. Christianity has defeated itself in that it has become a cultural thing. There really aren't believing Christians in the way there were generations ago.

DAWKINS: Certainly in Europe that's true—but in America?

HITCHENS: There are revivals, of course, and among Jews as well. But I think there's a very long-running tendency in the developed world and in large areas elsewhere for people to see the virtue of secularism, the separation of church and state, because they've tried the alternatives . . . Every time something like a jihad or a sharia movement has taken over any country—admittedly they've only been able to do it in very primitive cases—it's a smouldering wreck with no productivity.

DAWKINS: Total failure. If you look at religiosity across countries of the world and, indeed, across the states of the US, you find that religiosity tends to correlate with poverty and with various other indices of social deprivation.

HITCHENS: Yes. That's also what it feeds on. But I don't want to condescend about that. I know a lot of very educated, very prosperous, very thoughtful people who believe.

DAWKINS: Do you think [Thomas] Jefferson and [James] Madison were deists, as is often said?

HITCHENS: I think they fluctuated, one by one. Jefferson is the one I'm more happy to pronounce on. The furthest he would go in public was to incline to a theistic enlightened view but, in his private correspondence, he goes much further. He says he wishes we could return to the wisdom of more than 2,000 years ago. That's in his discussion of his own Jefferson Bible, where he cuts out everything supernatural relating to Jesus. But also, very importantly, he says to his nephew Peter Carr in a private letter [on the subject of belief]: "Do not be frightened from this inquiry by any fear of its consequences. If it ends in a belief that there is no God, you will find incitements to virtue in the comfort and pleasantness you feel in its exercise and the love of others which it will procure you." Now, that can only be written by someone who's had that experience.

DAWKINS: It's very good, isn't it?

HITCHENS: In my judgement, it's an internal reading, but I think it's a close one. There was certainly no priest at his bedside. But he did violate a rule of C. S. Lewis's and here I'm on Lewis's side. Lewis says it is a cop-out to say Jesus was a great moralist. He said it's the one thing we must not say; it is a wicked thing to say. If he wasn't the Son of God, he was a very evil impostor and his teachings were vain and fraudulent. You may not take the easy route here and say: "He may not have been the Son of God and he may not have been the Redeemer, but he was a wonderful moralist." Lewis is more honest than Jefferson in this point. I admire Lewis for saying that. Rick Perry said it the other day.

DAWKINS: Jesus could just have been mistaken.

HITCHENS: He could. It's not unknown for people to have the illusion that they're God or the Son. It's a common delusion but, again, I don't think we need to condescend. Rick Perry once said: "Not only do I believe that Jesus is my personal saviour but I believe that those who don't are going to eternal punishment." He was challenged at least on the last bit and he said, "I don't have the right to alter the doctrine. I can't say it's fine for me and not for others."

DAWKINS: So we ought to be on the side of these fundamentalists?

HITCHENS: Not "on the side," but I think we should say that there's something about their honesty that we wish we could find.

DAWKINS: Which we don't get in bishops . . .

HITCHENS: Our soft-centred bishops at Oxford and other people, yes.

DAWKINS: I'm often asked why it is that this republic [of America], founded in secularism, is so much more religious than those western European countries that have an official state religion, like Scandinavia and Britain.

HITCHENS: [Alexis] de Tocqueville has it exactly right. If you want a church in America, you have to build it by the sweat of your own brow, and many have. That's why they're attached to them.

DAWKINS: Yes.

HITCHENS: [Look at] the Greek Orthodox community in Brooklyn. What's the first thing it will do? It will build itself a little shrine. The Jews—not all of them—remarkably abandoned their religion very soon after arriving from the shtetl.

DAWKINS: Are you saying that most Jews have abandoned their religion?

HITCHENS: Increasingly in America. When you came to

escape religious persecution and you didn't want to replicate it, that's a strong memory. The Jews very quickly secularised when they came. American Jews must be the most secular force on the planet now, as a collective. If they are a collective—which they're not, really.

DAWKINS: While not being religious, they often still observe the Sabbath and that kind of thing.

HITCHENS: There's got to be something cultural. I go to Passover every year. Sometimes, even I have a seder, because I want my child to know that she does come very distantly from another tradition. It would explain if she met her great-grandfather why he spoke Yiddish. It's cultural, but the Passover seder is also the Socratic forum. It's dialectical. It's accompanied by wine. It's got the bones of quite a good discussion in it. And then there is manifest destiny. People feel America is just so lucky. It's between two oceans, filled with minerals, wealth, beauty. It does seem providential to many people.

DAWKINS: Promised land, city on a hill.

HITCHENS: All that and the desire for another Eden. Some secular utopians came here with the same idea. Thomas Paine and others all thought of America as a great new start for the species.

DAWKINS: But that was all secular.

HITCHENS: A lot of it was, but you can't get away from the liturgy: it's too powerful. You will end up saying things like "promised land" and it can be mobilised for sinister purposes. But in a lot of cases, it's a mild belief. It's just: "We should share our good luck."

DAWKINS: I've heard another theory that, America being a country of immigrants, people coming from Europe, where they left their extended family and left their support system, were alone and they needed something.

HITCHENS: Surely that was contained in what I just . . .

DAWKINS: Maybe it was.

HITCHENS: The reason why most of my friends are non-believers is not particularly that they were engaged in the arguments you and I have been having, but they were made indifferent by compulsory religion at school.

DAWKINS: They got bored by it.

HITCHENS: They'd had enough of it. They took from it occasionally whatever they needed—if you needed to get married, you knew where to go. Some of them, of course, are religious and some of them like the music but, generally speaking, the British people are benignly indifferent to religion.

DAWKINS: And the fact that there is an established church increases that effect. Churches should not be tax-free the way that they are. Not automatically, anyway.

HITCHENS: No, certainly not. If the Church has demanded that equal time be given to creationist or pseudo-creationist speculations . . . any Church that teaches that in its school and is in receipt of federal money from the faith-based initiative must, by law, also teach Darwinism and alternative teachings, in order that the debate is being taught. I don't think they want this.

DAWKINS: No.

HITCHENS: Tell them if they want equal time, we'll jolly well have it. That's why they've always been against comparative religion.

DAWKINS: Comparative religion would be one of the best weapons, I suspect.

HITCHENS: It's got so insipid in parts of America now that a lot of children are brought up—as their parents aren't doing it and leave it to the schools and the schools are afraid of it—with no knowledge of any religion of any kind. I would like children to know what religion is about because [otherwise] some guru or cult or revivalists will sweep them up.

DAWKINS: They're vulnerable. I also would like them to know the Bible for literary reasons.

HITCHENS: Precisely. We both, I was pleased to see, have written pieces about the King James Bible. The AV

[Authorised Version], as it was called in my boyhood. A huge amount of English literature would be opaque if people didn't know it.

DAWKINS: Absolutely, yes. Have you read some of the modern translations? "Futile, said the preacher. Utterly futile."

HITCHENS: He doesn't!

DAWKINS: He does, honestly. "Futile, futile said the priest. It's all futile."

HITCHENS: That's Lamentations.

DAWKINS: No, it's Ecclesiastes. "Vanity, vanity."

HITCHENS: "Vanity, vanity." Good God. That's the least religious book in the Bible. That's the one that Orwell wanted at his funeral.

DAWKINS: I bet he did. I sometimes think the poetry comes from the intriguing obscurity of mistranslation. "When the sound of the grinding is low, the grasshopper is heard in the land . . . The grasshopper shall be a burden." What the hell?

HITCHENS: The Book of Job is the other great non-religious one, I always feel. "Man is born to trouble as the sparks fly upward." Try to do without that. No, I'm glad we're on the same page there. People tell me that the recitation of the Quran can have the same effect if you understand the original language. I wish I did. Some of the Catholic liturgy is attractive.

DAWKINS: I don't know enough Latin to judge that.

HITCHENS: Sometimes one has just enough to be irritated.

DAWKINS: Yes [laughs]. Can you say anything about Christmas?

HITCHENS: Yes. There was going to be a winter solstice holiday for sure. The dominant religion was going to take it over and that would have happened without Dickens and without others.

DAWKINS: The Christmas tree comes from Prince Albert; the shepherds and the wise men are all made up.

HITCHENS: Cyrenius wasn't governor of Syria, all of that. Increasingly, it's secularised itself. This "Happy Holidays"—I don't particularly like that, either.

DAWKINS: Horrible, isn't it? "Happy holiday season."

HITCHENS: I prefer our stuff about the cosmos.

* * *

The day after this interview, I was honoured to present an award to Christopher Hitchens in the presence of a large audience in

Texas that gave him a standing ovation, first as he entered the hall and again at the end of his deeply moving speech. My own presentation speech ended with a tribute, in which I said that every day he demonstrates the falsehood of the lie that there are no atheists in foxholes: "Hitch is in a foxhole, and he is dealing with it with a courage, an honesty and a dignity that any of us would be, and should be, proud to muster."

CHRISTOPHER HITCHENS was an English-born American writer, essayist, and journalist, as well as an outspoken atheist. He began his writing career in England as a correspondent for a socialist publication before writing for *New Statesman*. He then moved to the United States in 1981 and became an editor for *The Nation*. In 1992 he joined *Vanity Fair* as a contributing editor and he stayed with the publication for the remainder of his life. He also wrote a monthly column for *The Atlantic*, contributed regularly to *The New York Review of Books*, appeared as a talking head on countless television shows, and wrote or co-authored seventeen books. Hitchens also taught as a visiting professor at the University of California Berkeley and a liberal studies professor at the New School. In 2010 he was diagnosed with esophageal cancer, though this did not slow him down much as he continued to write and give interviews until he died on December 15, 2011.

STEPHEN FRY is an English actor, screenwriter, author, playwright, journalist, poet, comedian, television presenter, and film director. As half of the comic double act Fry and Laurie, he co-wrote and co-starred *in A Bit of Fry & Laurie*, and took the role of Jeeves (with Hugh Laurie playing Wooster) in *Jeeves and Wooster*. In addition to his years of work in film and television, Fry has contributed columns and articles for newspapers and magazines, appears frequently on radio, reads for voice-overs and has written four novels and three volumes of autobiography, *Moab Is My Washpot*, *The Fry Chronicles*, and *More Fool Me*. His latest book is *Mythos*.

CARL RUTAN was a political editor with C-Span from 1982 to 1989, hosting viewer call-in segments and other weekly programs. He is the television producer of *Grassroots '84*, *March on Washington: Commemoration of Martin Luther King's '63 March*, and *Teacher TV*—the latter of which he also wrote. Rutan was awarded a Capital Regional Emmy Award, which honors individuals in local news, for his segments on public affairs.

MATT CHERRY is the Executive Director of Death Penalty Focus and Executive Vice President of Cherry Communications. A professional leader within the humanist movements of the UK, the Netherlands, and the United States, Cherry's passion for humanist work led him to serve as the president of the United Nations Non-Government Organizations Committee on Freedom of Religion or Belief. He has also worked as a Representative of the International Humanist and Ethical Union, and was the Executive Director of both the Institute for Humanist Studies and the Council for Secular Humanism.

SASHA ABRAMSKY is a freelance journalist. His work has appeared in numerous publications including *The Nation*, *Slate*, and *The Atlantic*. Abramsky is the author of several critically acclaimed books, the latest of which is a memoir titled *The House of Twenty Thousand Books*.

J. C. GABEL is the founder of the magazine *Stop Smiling* and Stop Smiling Books. He was the editorial and creative director for the 2012 revival of *The Chicagoan* and is the current editor and associate publisher for *The Pitchfork Review*. His articles have appeared in *The Wall Street Journal, Playboy, Bookforum, The LA Times, The New York Times,* and *Wallpaper*. He also cofounded the Los Angeles-based publishing house and print collective Hat & Beard Press.

JAMES HUGHES is the former managing editor and co-publisher for the magazine *Stop Smiling* and its book imprint, Stop Smiling Books. His writing has appeared in *The Atlantic, Grantland, Slate, Film Comment, The Paris Review, The Village Voice,* and *The Believer*.

JON STEWART is a writer, filmmaker, actor, comedian, and the former host of *The Daily Show*. Stewart's political satire earned *The Daily Show* two Peabody Awards and twenty Primetime Emmy Awards during his sixteen-year tenure. He coauthored *America (The Book): A Citizen's Guide to Democracy Inaction* in 2004 and *Earth (The Book): A Visitor's Guide to the Human Race* in 2010. Stewart also wrote, directed, and produced the 2014 film *Rosewater*.

MARILYN SEWELL is a former teacher and psychotherapist and the author of numerous books. She served as the Senior Minister for the First Unitarian Church of Portland, Oregon for seventeen years. Sewell currently is a contributor for *Huffington Post* and a poetry editor for *The Harvard Divinity Bulletin*.

ANDREW ANTHONY has been writing for *Observer* since 1993 and for *The Guardian* since 1990. He is the author of *On Penalties*, published by Yellow Jersey Press, and *The Fallout*, published by Jonathan Cape.

RICHARD DAWKINS is a prominent scientist and an icon within the secular movement. He is an internationally best-selling author of numerous books, the most recent of which is an autobiography, *Brief Candle in the Dark: My Life in Science*. Dawkins is a Fellow of both the Royal Society and the Royal Society of Literature, as well as an Emeritus Fellow of the New College, Oxford. He was also the University of Oxford's Professor for Public Understanding of Science for thirteen years.

THE LAST INTERVIEW SERIES

KURT VONNEGUT: THE LAST INTERVIEW

"I think it can be tremendously refreshing if a creator of literature has something on his mind other than the history of literature so far. Literature should not disappear up its own asshole, so to speak."

$15.95 / $17.95 CAN
978-1-61219-090-7
ebook: 978-1-61219-091-4

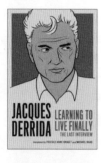

LEARNING TO LIVE FINALLY: THE LAST INTERVIEW
JACQUES DERRIDA

"I am at war with myself, it's true, you couldn't possibly know to what extent . . . I say contradictory things that are, we might say, in real tension; they are what construct me, make me live, and will make me die."

translated by PASCAL-ANNE BRAULT and MICHAEL NAAS

$15.95 / $17.95 CAN
978-1-61219-094-5

ROBERTO BOLAÑO: THE LAST INTERVIEW

"Posthumous: It sounds like the name of a Roman gladiator, an unconquered gladiator. At least that's what poor Posthumous would like to believe. It gives him courage."

translated by SYBIL PEREZ and others

$15.95 / $17.95 CAN
978-1-61219-095-2
ebook: 978-1-61219-033-4

DAVID FOSTER WALLACE: THE LAST INTERVIEW

"I don't know what you're thinking or what it's like inside you and you don't know what it's like inside me. In fiction . . . we can leap over that wall itself in a certain way."

$15.95 / $15.95 CAN
978-1-61219-206-2
ebook: 978-1-61219-207-9

THE LAST INTERVIEW SERIES

JORGE LUIS BORGES: THE LAST INTERVIEW

"Believe me: the benefits of blindness have been greatly exaggerated. If I could see, I would never leave the house, I'd stay indoors reading the many books that surround me."

translated by KIT MAUDE

$15.95 / $15.95 CAN
978-1-61219-204-8
ebook: 978-1-61219-205-5

HANNAH ARENDT: THE LAST INTERVIEW

"There are no dangerous thoughts for the simple reason that thinking itself is such a dangerous enterprise."

$15.95 / $15.95 CAN
978-1-61219-311-3
ebook: 978-1-61219-312-0

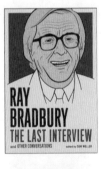

RAY BRADBURY: THE LAST INTERVIEW

"You don't have to destroy books to destroy a culture. Just get people to stop reading them."

$15.95 / $15.95 CAN
978-1-61219-421-9
ebook: 978-1-61219-422-6

JAMES BALDWIN: THE LAST INTERVIEW

"You don't realize that you're intelligent until it gets you into trouble."

$15.95 / $15.95 CAN
978-1-61219-400-4
ebook: 978-1-61219-401-1